PRAISE FOR *COPING APPROACHES FROM S(*

"*Coping with Educational Crises: Approaches from School Leaders Who Did It!* is an important read for practitioners and academics alike as we emerge from the COVID-19 pandemic. The insights provided by the authors are incredibly relevant as they share lessons learned. They encourage us to explore how we, as educators, have a critically important role to play in navigating the turbulent forces of change during crisis. Dr. Polka and his colleagues do an exceptional job of exploring the full spectrum of leadership challenges during a global crisis from the unique perspective of school leaders. Their stories help us to understand how they seized the opportunity to pivot during the most difficult of times and to marshal in a new era of school leadership post-pandemic through creativity, perseverance, and an unwavering commitment to students."

—Holly Catalfamo, EdD, director of global engagement,
Niagara College, Ontario, Canada

"Educational leaders face myriad anticipated and unanticipated challenges, many of which multiplied during the COVID-19 pandemic. *Coping with Educational Crises: Approaches from School Leaders Who Did It!* is a book full of experiences shared by top leaders, researchers, and practitioners on how to continue to navigate a current crisis situation as well as courageously prepare for an unknown future with researched strategies, confidence, and hopefulness. I highly endorse this resource for beginning and seasoned educational leaders at all levels and for researchers who care deeply about doing education right in times of both calm and turmoil."

—Angela Ford, EdD, assistant professor of educational
research, Judson University, Elgin, Illinois, and president
of the International Society for Educational Planning

"When the Covid pandemic hit our shores in 2020, most educators had very little time to prepare for how it was going to impact our schools, students, and teachers. *Coping with Educational Crises: Approaches from School Leaders Who Did It!* co-edited by Walter S. Polka, John E. McKenna, and Monica Jo VanHusen, provides examples from school leaders across the USA and Canada of approaches and programs put into place to deal with the pandemic's impact on schools. This is a must-read for educators to be prepared for the next 'crisis'—no matter how big or small—that may have an effect on our students and teachers."

—Dr. D. John McIntyre, professor emeritus and senior visiting
professor in curriculum studies, Southern Illinois University

"*Coping with Educational Crises: Approaches from School Leaders Who Did It!* is a well-thought-out book that provides a comprehensive look at the approach school leaders, at all levels, took with the COVID-19 pandemic. Stories are shared in detail, allowing leaders at all stages to read about this historical event, learn from it, and prepare for future crises as well as recognize the opportunities that may result from a crisis. Furthermore, this book provides a great perspective for all individuals of how schools and districts operate, providing insight on day-to-day operations and the considerations that need to be addressed during a crisis to ensure the needs of the school, community, and all stakeholders are met."

—Lori Fulton, PhD, professor, Institute for Teacher
Education, University of Hawai'i at Manoa

"We often hear that timing is everything. This book fits that motto well, as its timing is a perfect fit for the leader who seeks knowledge from those in the field who dealt firsthand with a once-in-a-century challenge. This book has something for all educators regardless of their position in education and does what we all should do: learn from, quite possibly, the biggest challenge a leader will face. Experience the challenge through the eyes of leaders who dealt with the pandemic at the ground level. Learn from these brave leaders as they share their experiences and thoughts on not only the pandemic, but the future of education."

—Dr. Paul M. Fanuele, superintendent of schools,
Spackenkill Union Free School District

"This timely publication offers practical perspectives and useful concepts, brought forward by the admirable and immensely useful chapters in *Coping with Educational Crises: Approaches from School Leaders Who Did It!* is an invaluable resource for *on the ground* and *in the weeds* active participation in school leadership, providing the reality of experiential practice and embedded voice with continuously constructive nuggets of practical advice related to community-support, ethics, and integrity. This publication is equally valuable to researchers focused upon educational leadership, as well as organizational leadership, performance improvement, change management, and human resources from an organizational psychology perspective. As the tumultuous 21st century rolls forward, this publication will become even more important and may well reach the status of a guidebook beacon towards dealing with forthcoming major crises in the schools."

—Caroline M. Crawford, EdD, professor, Instructional Design
and Technology, University of Houston–Clear Lake

"The coronavirus has had a devastating and disruptive impact on organizations and has created unprecedented challenges for leaders in every domain. As the director of a graduate leadership program, I found this book: *Coping with Educational Crises: Approaches from School Leaders Who Did It!* to be an excellent resource for leaders and especially for leadership graduate students. Each chapter provides insightful, evidence-based guiding practices aimed at not just leading, but leading WELL in the world, even during a crisis. I really appreciate the emphasis on ethics and humanity as we navigate a post pandemic future."

—Kimberly DeSimone, PhD, professor and director of the Master's in Leadership Program, St. Bonaventure University

"If leaders want to thrive in the time of crises, this book, *Coping with Educational Crises: Approaches from School Leaders Who Did It!* provides passionate, yet practical, insights from the experience of leaders who in their time of turmoil and crises were able to successfully facilitate educational programs and processes in their respective school contexts. Each chapter is filled with trends, testaments, reviews, studies, and/or strategies that spark reassurance and confidence in leaders, reminding them they can make it through any challenge, even during a pandemic, epidemic, and endemic. This book is important to have readily available on the practitioner's professional desk not just in the bookcase because it serves as a powerful resource that shows educators and stakeholders how educational leaders coped and thrived during this most unprecedented and turbulent time in education."

—Jennifer K. Young Wallace, PhD, associate professor of educational leadership and coordinator of K–12 PhD program, Jackson State University

Coping with
Educational Crises

Coping with Educational Crises

Approaches from School Leaders Who Did It

Edited by
Walter S. Polka
John E. McKenna
Monica J. VanHusen

ROWMAN & LITTLEFIELD
Lanham • Boulder • New York • London

Published by Rowman & Littlefield
An imprint of The Rowman & Littlefield Publishing Group, Inc.
4501 Forbes Boulevard, Suite 200, Lanham, Maryland 20706
www.rowman.com
86-90 Paul Street, London EC2A 4NE, United Kingdom

British Library Cataloguing in Publication Information Available

Library of Congress Cataloging-in-Publication Data

Names: Polka, Walter S., 1945– editor. | McKenna, John, 1963– editor. | VanHusen,
    Monica J., 1980– editor.
Title: Coping with educational crises : approaches from school leaders who did it /
    edited by Walter S. Polka, John E. McKenn, Monica J. VanHusen.
Description: Lanham, Maryland : Rowman & Littlefield, [2023] |
    Includes bibliographical references. | Summary: "Coping with Educational
    Crises: Approaches from School Leaders Who Did It provides key leadership concepts
    and specific strategies as well as pragmatic tactical approaches that school
    leaders must employ to successfully confront the realities of crises situations and
    appropriately lead their followers into the post-crisis experience"—Provided by
    publisher.
Identifiers: LCCN 2022048616 (print) | LCCN 2022048617 (ebook) |
    ISBN 9781475865943 (Cloth) | ISBN 9781475865950 (Paperback)
    | ISBN 9781475865967 (epub)
Subjects: LCSH: Educational leadership—United States. | School administrators—
    Professional relationships—United States. | School management and organization—
    United States. | Crisis management—United States.
Classification: LCC LB2805 .C65918 2023 (print) | LCC LB2805 (ebook) |
    DDC 371.2/0110973—dc23/eng/20221108
LC record available at https://lccn.loc.gov/2022048616
LC ebook record available at https://lccn.loc.gov/2022048617

This book is dedicated to ALL school leaders who addressed the most impactful educational crisis of our time: COVID-19. They individually and collectively strived to maintain quality education during catastrophic conditions that deleteriously impacted the foundations of education and our society. Thank you for your ardent dedication to education and your unwavering support of your students and faculty. You all made a difference in teaching and learning in our global village to enable schools to effectively function and even flourish in very difficult situations.

This book is also dedicated to our family members, who also exemplified dedication and support to us as we embarked on this journey of amassing the history of this crisis and assembling this book as a reference for current and future school leaders. Specifically, we wish to dedicate this work to our immediate family members:

John E. McKenna's family members:
Caroline McKenna
Matthew McKenna
Daniel McKenna
Mark McKenna
Emily Lacy
Walter S. Polka's family members:
Victoria M. Polka
Jennifer M. Polka Sommerfield
Jeffrey Sommerfield
Hunter Sommerfield
Monica Jo VanHusen
Nathan VanHusen
Connor VanHusen
Victoria VanHusen
We thank you ALL for your love and support!

Contents

Foreword

March 2020 is a time we will all never forget for many personal and professional reasons. In our education profession, schools had to quickly figure out how to transfer from in-person learning, something they had been used to for well over a century, to pandemic teaching and learning. It was referred to as pandemic teaching and learning because there were many schools around the world that had never engaged in deep remote learning experiences for students.

In April of 2020, UNESCO reported that 82 percent of the world's student population were forced to go to remote learning due to COVID-19. This brought monumental challenges for many schools, regardless of whether they were suburban, rural, or urban.

There were many issues that came to light, some of which were the impact of poverty and the need for social-emotional learning. I remember doing remote walkthroughs with leaders I coach, and students would have their cameras on engaging in learning at the same time they were holding their baby siblings.

I have to admit, the fact that issues of poverty and mental health took COVID-19 to come to light was somewhat frustrating. We know that Kozol focused on the impact of poverty back in the 1990s, and within my own Finding Common Ground blog, I have written about the need for social-emotional learning over the more than eleven years the blog has been in existence.

And yet, for most of those years leading up to COVID-19, social-emotional learning was the topic where I received the most pushback from readers, and many of those readers were educators. They used to say that we don't have time for social-emotional learning, and then after COVID-19, those very people were screaming, "Maslow before Bloom!"

However, the good news is that due to unprecedented national and international news coverage, people began to see all of the challenges that schools have faced long before COVID-19 entered into our lives. Additionally, due to that news coverage, people were exposed to the deep relationships between schools and their communities, as well as the fact that there are no bounds that will get in the way of what teachers and leaders will do for their students.

During those first few months of COVID-19, we saw school leaders, teachers, and the rest of the school community engaging in extraordinary actions. In most areas, we know that schools are the hubs for so much, and COVID-19 showed all of the ways that schools served their communities.

In some high-poverty schools in California where I coach, there were high schools serving over one-thousand lunches per day, and the county offices sent out city busses that were equipped with Wi-Fi to different parts of town so that students could have access for a few hours a day.

These, of course, are just a few of the countless examples of humanity that school leaders showed during the over two years of COVID-19, which leads me to this very important book that you are about to read: *Coping with Educational Crises: Approaches from School Leaders Who Did It!* Polka, McKenna, and VanHusen have created an important piece of reading for all of us, because they have edited stories from leaders who had to learn how to pivot every single day and lead their school communities through the most challenging time that schools will probably ever see in our lifetime.

What we also know is that the challenges of schools are not over. As I write this, we still have deep political polarization playing out in our classrooms and schools. Flags are being waved, books are being banned, and mental health is still a national issue. We need not read these chapters with just a COVID lens, but also should read these chapters with a lens of how we can come together through our political and mental health issues, too.

As much as these stories are about leading through a pandemic, they are more than that as well, because these stories are also about leading. When reading this book, don't just look at each chapter as a reflection on leading in a time of COVID-19; use them as a roadmap to help you lead through the future as well. These stories are a how-to on how to engage a community during any time, which we know can also help us lead during any time.

Peter DeWitt, EdD
Author/Education Week Blogger/Leadership Coach/Workshop Facilitator
https://en.unesco.org/covid19/educationresponse#schoolclosures

Preface

John E. McKenna, Walter S. Polka, and Monica J. VanHusen

This book provides readers with practical perspectives and research-based strategies regarding the leadership approaches employed by school district administrators at all levels—including superintendents of schools, assistant superintendents, program directors, coordinators, principals, assistant principals, and teacher leaders—of organizational responsibility to confront a crisis, such as the one created by the COVID-19 global pandemic commencing in spring 2020.

The book consists of eight chapters written by practicing administrators, leadership researchers, and experienced educators who present their analyses and insights about managing the "people things," and ideas of educational organizations during crisis situations. They uniquely articulate various well-researched approaches that they and other educational leaders employed to abate the deleterious impact of crises on their respective organizations.

They also provide pragmatic recommendations to current and future school leaders, based on their experiences and research, who may face similar crises during their careers. In addition, they provide sage advice to current educational policy-makers, school administrators, parents, and community leaders to recognize the collateral opportunities associated with any crisis including reforms to the pre-crisis traditional educational system since some of its key foundations, procedures, and expectations have been significantly changed.

The chapter authors are current or former practitioners who have been actively engaged in school leadership experiences as well as action research related to improving schools and administrative approaches. They provide readers with acute perspectives of their experiences managing themselves and others through this most recent global cataclysmic crisis. They represent

xvi   *Preface*
educational leaders who toiled daily to survive and help their schooling contexts, especially their students, survive and thrive through this turbulent period in our history.

This book was developed to give those who experienced this crisis the opportunity to share their leadership stories from personal, professional, and organizational perspectives. They want their "voices" and those of their colleagues' experiences about this unprecedented, punctuated COVID-19 crisis heard, as well as to explain its detrimental impact upon the people, things, and ideas of their respective educational organizations.

These ten practicing leaders employ their action research skills, professional reflections, and eclectic organizational position perspectives to tell their robust stories of personal and organizational survival during this recent global crisis and to recommend actions for educational leaders who may be confronted with similar unanticipated major crises in the future.

The book gives meaningful "voice" to the authors and their colleagues who possessed different leadership roles in their organizations, but, carried out their assigned tasks with expediency and efficacy during this historical crisis in order to preserve the cultural essence of schooling. Their stories will resonate with readers as they review the maelstrom of issues associated with fulfilling leadership roles and expectations during such a detrimental global event as COVID-19.

Practical advice is presented in each chapter about how leaders, who are still in spotlighted educational leadership roles, are able to successfully manage themselves and others, not only through the turbulence caused by the COVID-19 crisis but also through the impact of its wake on the traditional institution of schooling in America. Some perceive that this event may galvanize segments of communities into special interest groups and foment real reforms in teaching and learning based on our inherent educational values and democratic traditions as well as sound research related to the needs and interests of our children.

There are several interesting opportunities for our educational system leaders to further evolve our systems for the better because of the fundamental structural, operational, and interpersonal havoc caused by this virus and our collective education leadership reactions to it in 2020, 2021, and 2022.

The leaders highlighted in this book posit their thoughts regarding key changes that they perceive should and could occur to improve education for all children. Readers are encouraged to remember that even in the "darkest" periods of human history, hope has sprung eternal, and humankind has developed even better systems than those wreaked by unexpected drastic events.

Acknowledgments

Walter S. Polka, John E. McKenna, and Monica J. VanHusen, as the editors of this collaborative publication effort, wish to thank key focused individuals who have contributed their time, energy, and leadership expertise to the completion of this book.

First and foremost, we wish to recognize the invaluable work of the authors of chapters in this book who have specifically provided their examples and reflections of their practical experiences of operating school programs and school districts during the most catastrophic educational experience of our time. They have each provided pertinent information as educational leaders who have managed people, things, and ideas under their supervision, regarding approaches to successfully confront the exigencies of a crisis and construct effective adaptions to normal school operations—especially teaching and learning—in order to promote the survival and thriving of the educational enterprise in their respective micro and macro contexts.

Their "lived experiences" as leaders during this specific global COVID-19 crisis are reflected in their chapters that include thoughts about their own personal experiences as well as those of their colleagues in similar organizational roles throughout the United States. Their strategic approaches, operational processes, communication procedures, and pragmatic artifacts such as faculty and student memos and parent informational documents serve as valuable resource models and templates. These documented experiences and pragmatic documents all contribute to the historical reference value of this book to current and aspiring school leaders who may also face a similar crisis in their careers. A very sincere thank you to: Carol S. Cash, Moira Cooper, Jodie Brinkmann, Michelle Grimes, Ruby Harris, Ted Price, and Jeffrey R. Rabey.

We know that your leadership experiences during this crisis as reflected in your specific chapters will serve as guiding practices and key references for other school leaders to consider when confronting planned or unplanned significant interruptions to their school operations, whether caused by natural or man-made crises, or a combination of both. It has been truly an outstanding professional opportunity to know and work with each one of you in completing this book. You are excellent educational leaders, and your stories of survival during this time period will resonate with other educational leaders well into the future!

In addition, the editors of this book wish to thank the following two individuals who have contributed their expertise in providing research and proofing services as well as book layout recommendations regarding this publication: Caroline McKenna and Molly Oliverio. We appreciate all of your efforts on our behalf!

Introduction

Walter S. Polka, John E. McKenna, and Monica J. VanHusen

This book reflects the practical approaches and actions of educational leaders who successfully managed their school operations and promoted teaching and learning during the recent COVID-19 crisis in various contexts. This book focuses on the "exemplary leadership practices" as portrayed by authors who had experiences in those leadership roles and who provide specific documentation to the decisions they made and the actions they advocated for their employees, students, and community.

The eight chapters in this book take the reader on an expedition through pragmatic experiences and research-based best practices related to successful leadership strategies and tactics that were implemented to address the ubiquitous COVID-19 crisis.

Each chapter provides critical information, knowledge, and specific steps that leaders have utilized to lead their organizations toward success in a crisis. The chapters in this book generally begin with a quote, vignette, or other analogies to motivate and set the stage for the reader. The authors use a variety of approaches in their chapter presentations to illustrate key aspects of the strategies and methods employed by school leaders in various supervisory roles and responsibilities.

At the end of each chapter there are both "Chapter Author(s) Final Thoughts" and "Key Pragmatic Leadership Takeaways" sections designed to reinforce the key leadership concepts included the chapter as well as to provide specific recommendations that educational leaders may use to address the deleterious impacts of any crisis, whether natural or man-made.

The following is a summary of each chapter and how they collectively convey a comprehensive roadmap for leaders to follow in any crisis situation:

Chapter 1. The authors of this chapter provide information collected from a qualitative survey of 137 school administrators from all supervisory education levels in Virginia and neighboring states. This chapter is more than a report of the data from the survey instrument administered over a six-week time period at the onset of the COVID-19 global pandemic. It includes specific themes with selected comments from respondents for emphasis and overarching findings as well as associated discussions related to the initial reactions and experiences of school administrators as they confronted this global pandemic.

Chapter 2. This chapter is a summary of a practicing superintendent's experiences during the global crisis, and it provides recommendations for preparing for the future. This chapter is written through the experiential lens of a practicing New York suburban superintendent who has been a superintendent of schools for over fifteen years. This chapter provides valuable historical documentation and analyses of crisis exigencies and school district leadership reactions to them during the first five months of COVID-19 in New York state.

The author provides very replicable communication procedures, memos, and other pragmatic artifacts that may be used by other school district leaders in similar triage-type chaos situations. The articulated strategies and examples provide a day-to-day-type approach to dealing with any unexpected micro-context crises that are often exacerbated by macro-level procedural inconsistencies.

Chapter 3. This chapter is a synthesized case study of the "lived, real-world administrative experiences" of educational leaders who served as administrators during the COVID-19 crisis, and their efforts after the first "shock of school closures" to develop a strategic plan and specific structures to re-open their schools for all students during the 2020–2021 school year. This chapter contains practical information related to the actions and reactions of school leaders who efficiently and effectively confronted the ongoing realities of the crisis as reflected in this amalgamated case study. This chapter provides a strategic framework for other school leaders to follow when confronted with similar crisis situations.

Chapter 4. The authors of this chapter identify how educational leaders who have a deep commitment to instructional improvements can "spark" building administrators and teachers that they supervise or coordinate to move toward collaborating, creating, and maintaining a responsive and reliable curriculum for students at any time, but most especially during crisis situations. The authors illustrate how leaders may intentionally build teacher efficacy and agency to create and facilitate responsive and reliable curricular and instructional practices that help students be prepared for their future.

Chapter 5. This chapter illuminates the myriad experiences of an assistant superintendent for school business and finance and her various trials and tribulations associated with maintaining the business of the school district during the pandemic, including food services for students, facilities maintenance, budget appropriations, and financial investments. She very specifically and quite cogently captures the significance of maintaining school operations with adequate support services and appropriate leadership focus.

Chapter 6. This chapter analyzes the issues, challenges, and dilemmas faced by human resources leaders during crises, such as the 2020 global pandemic, in dealing with regulations and mandates from state and local authorities. They examine the rules and regulations that interface with people who each possess unique needs and circumstances that must be considered when implementing human resource policies. The authors emphasize the importance of keeping the "human" in human resources, especially in uncertain times that exacerbate feelings of fear of the unknown and result in heightened issues of stress and anxiety on all employees.

Chapter 7. This chapter is based on leadership positions to which the author was appointed during the global pandemic that provided her with unique perspectives of managing people, things, and ideas as a relatively new leader in two different educational organizations in a unique time in history. The author is a senior administrator who has served as a faculty member and leader in the Ontario, Canada, college system for over fifteen years.

Chapter 8. In this chapter, the authors challenge educational leaders to develop a growth mindset and create a new and better educational system for all in the future. Their analysis is based on shared collective experiences of administrators during the COVID-19 crisis. The authors contend that educational leaders must adroitly review and critically analyze the impact of the crisis on teaching and learning and determine the next "best-fit" options for faculty and students. The authors also assert that leaders must have the courage to identify and steadfastly pursue a preferable future of education for all.

The editors of this book certainly hope that you enjoy the reviews and analyses of the "lived experiences" of practicing school leaders who had unbridled commitment, inexhaustible creativity, focused sense of challenge, and incredible caring approaches to confront the unexpected COVID-19 global crisis in their organizational contexts and promote the continuation of school operations including innovative changes in the delivery of services to their students and parents.

The leaders referenced in the chapters of this book are, indeed, twenty-first-century education trailblazers whose experiences, examples, and recommendations pragmatically established unique and interesting operational paths for coping with crises that other leaders may wish to heed and pursue in their future.

Chapter 1

School Leadership in a Global Crisis

A Study of Initial Reactions and Future Perspectives

Carol S. Cash, Jodie L. Brinkmann, and Ted S. Price

"Children are the world's most valuable resource and its best hope for the future."

—John F. Kennedy, thirty-fifth president

As the projected end of the coronavirus crisis nears, or at least as people return to a more normal environment, it is important to remember the early days and the challenges that school leaders predicted and to which they responded. The study described below was conducted in the early days of the COVID-19 pandemic, and recorded accurate and timely leadership reactions to the crisis. This chapter focuses on the impact of the coronavirus on school leadership, but the recommendations consider equity in light of both challenges, social unrest, and the coronavirus. The call for courageous leadership is as vital now as it has ever been.

As 2020 began, so did an event that was both unexpected and disruptive. The coronavirus pandemic emerged with a few localized infections in China and then spread throughout the world over the next several months. The United States began to feel its impact in the early months of 2020, with pre-K–12 schools beginning to close in early March. By the end of March, all states had either mandated or recommended the closing of schools, with the vast majority of those schools continuing their closures throughout the school year.

As the first schools closed, a team of educational leadership professors at Virginia Tech began to consider the impact of these closures on public education in their region of the United States and on its leaders, at both the school and central office levels. It was important to document the reactions and thoughts of leaders at the beginning of the pandemic. There is value in recording an event as it occurs in order to avoid revisionist history, which can occur when one looks back at an event after it has occurred.

It is well documented that leadership is crucial to moving forward—to facilitating the change process and change itself. Thus, asking leaders to share their thoughts provided a map for progress and change. In March 2020, shortly after schools in the United States closed because of the coronavirus, this research team felt compelled to learn more about perceptions of school administrators and the impact of the coronavirus on education and their community. Using a qualitative survey and snowballing for sampling and distribution, this team collected responses from 137 school leaders. The demographic questions were collected as indicated below.

Who are you (What position do you hold in your school division/district)?

- Elementary principal
- Elementary assistant principal
- Middle school principal
- Middle school assistant principal
- High school principal
- High school assistant principal
- Central office administrator
- Other

Please indicate in which state you work as an administrator:

- Virginia
- North Carolina
- Florida
- Other

The qualitative open responses posed to the participants addressed the following questions:

- What was your first thought when you heard about the coronavirus?
- What was your first priority when the closing of schools was announced?

/hat has been your communication, formal and informal, with your takeholders?

- What would you want to tell the students who are in their final grade at your level—should they end the year without returning?
- What is your reaction to the canceling of state tests for this school year?
- How do you see this interruption impacting future classes and students?
- What is your opinion of how school year grades should be finalized if students don't return to school?
- As we *capture this moment in time* what else should we record?

The survey was distributed throughout the Commonwealth of Virginia and other neighboring states using snowballing methods, and participant responses were collected over the next six weeks. The analysis of data, using qualitative methodology, provided a snapshot of leaders' perceptions and the impact of the coronavirus on their school, staff, students, and community. In this paper, the top three themes that emerged from school level leadership are provided.

Of the 137 respondents, 36 were from the central office (CO), 48 were from the elementary level (E), 20 were from the middle level (M), and 27 were from the high school level (H). There were 6 respondents who indicated (other). Those responses are not being considered in this disaggregated reporting of the data. The respondents came from Virginia (n=128), North Carolina (n=1), and other states (n=8).

This chapter, however, is more than a report of the data from the survey. It includes specific themes with selected comments for emphasis from study sample participants, and overarching findings as well as associated discussion. Finally, a Post-Hoc Focus Panel of experienced school leaders articulated their perceptions about how these findings could lead to changes in PK-12 education.

INITIAL TOP THREE THEMES BY SCHOOL LEVEL

In this section, each of the open-ended questions are presented and the top three response themes from each school level are be shared. Following the identification of those themes a few illustrative participant responses are identified.

What Was Your First Thought When You Heard About the Coronavirus?

Central office respondents for this study (n=36), identified that the top responses fell under the theme *played down* (n=13). The next highest theme related to *having questions* (n=7), and the third theme by rank indicated that this was *serious* (n=4). The following are representative comments from the study participants regarding their initial thoughts about COVID-19:

> America will be better prepared than China. What happened in China will never happen here.
> That this was a concern that probably would not have a great deal of impact on the US.
> How hard will it hit us and are we prepared?
> COVID-19 was something to take seriously.

The elementary respondents (n=48) more frequently dismissed concerns, with their most frequently mentioned theme being that they *didn't expect this to impact the U.S.* (n=24) followed by *played down* (n=13), with the third most frequent response indicating they felt it was going to similar to the *flu* (n=11). Accordingly, representative comments from these elementary administrators are as follows:

> I saw it transpiring in China, but did not think it was coming to the U.S.A.
> I initially didn't think anything of it.
> It was like the flu. Wash your hands. You may get it, you may not. Not a big deal.
> My first thought was that we would get through this just like we do flu season.

The highest frequency of response item from the middle school respondents (n=19) was played *down* (n=7) followed by *concern* (n=5). The third most frequently identified theme was *didn't expect this to impact the U.S.* (n=3). Representative responses from middle school administrators included:

> I was not overly concerned when I first heard because at that point it was in Asia only (as far as we knew) so it was business as usual.
> How can we keep our community safe from the virus?
> I didn't feel it would impact the US and certainly the education system to the level that it has.

Within the group of high school respondents (n=27), the most frequent response (n=10) fell under the theme of *concern/serious*. The next three most frequent responses had equal frequency (n=6) and included *didn't expect this* to impact the *U.S., played down,* and similar to the *flu.* The following are representative comments from the high school administrators:

Because of my background in public health, I thought it had the potential to be the next pandemic.

This is serious. I wonder if or when it will affect the US.

With a science background, I knew we may be in trouble when it was first seen in China.

My first thought was that it's just another virus, similar to the flu.

That it would be like any of the other viruses we have had to deal with as a human society, and it wouldn't impact us here in the U.S.

What Was Your First Priority When the Closing of Schools Was Announced?

The central office respondents identified that the top responses fell under the theme *learning* (n=15). The next highest theme identified related to *food* (n=10), and the third theme by ranked by them was *support, both for teachers/staff and for students* (n=8). The following selected responses from central office administrators fall under those themes.

Our initial closing was for only 2 weeks. At that time, our three focus areas were: (1) Continuity of meals for economically disadvantaged students; (2) Engaging students in learning while we were out of the buildings; (3) Deep cleaning all facilities in preparation for a return.

How will we continue to educate the children at all levels knowing that some of the students will not have the needed supports in their household.

Our first priority was to set up a meals program so that we could provide lunch to the children of our county.

Feeding our students.

My first priority was the health and safety of my staff, which rivaled with that of the students we serve.

The elementary leaders most frequently responded by identifying the theme of *support, for students and staff* (n=12), followed by *learning* (n=11), with the third most frequent response being, *communication* (n=10). The next theme selected was *food* (n=9), which is important to mention, as it is closely related to top theme of *support.* The following selected comments reflect those feelings of the elementary administrators:

I have tried to be very deliberate in how we have been asking staff to complete tasks that need to be done so that they are not overwhelmed.

Getting accurate information to staff and parents. Developing a system of communication for the closure. Having a plan for how to execute the closure.

Getting parents information, sending work home for the students and reassuring the teachers were my first priorities.

My first priority was making sure there was a plan in place to ensure that our students were fed.

My first priority was to make sure that students were still able to learn.

At first, I thought about my staff.

The highest frequency of response them from the middle school respondents to this question was, *communication* (n=6), followed by *food* (n=5) and *safety* (n=5). Accordingly, the following comments reflect their focus:

Communication with staff, community, students.

Making sure we have a means to get food and resources for our students.

Keeping students safe and making sure they understood we were there for them.

The group of high school administrators who responded to this question, identified that the most frequent response (n=8) fell under the theme of *communication.* The next two most frequent responses had equal frequency (n=7) and included *learning* and *support:*

Staying connected with our students, families, and staff.

First priority was how was instruction going to continue for the students.

The first thing was to be there for students and teachers. Assisting in planning for instruction online as well as lending an ear in uncertain times was necessary.

What Has Been Your Communication, Formal and Informal, With Your Stakeholders?

While this question was asked of each representative school level of leadership, the responses from all groups indicated a variety of communication tools including social media and print materials as reflected in the following comments:

Auto dials, social media, phone conversation, email, In person discussions. (H)

Call outs by phone, mass emails, teachers making weekly contact with students and parents, using virtual meeting formats for Special Education meetings with families. (M)

District letters and phone messengers, PTO Facebook page, Dojo, website, Google classroom, phone messengers, email, phone calls. (E)

Emailed memos, posting memos to website, social media, zoom meetings with faculty and staff (CO)

What Would You Want to Tell the Students Who Are in Their Final Grade at Your Level—Should They End the Year Without Returning?

While each level had unique situations, with the high school changes in the graduation process being the most drastic, their responses were often quite similar.

The central office personnel, provided a more comprehensive pre-K–12 viewpoint, by indicating their *encouragement* (n=8), and *support* (n=6), as well as *recognition that this situation was unique* (n=6). The following selected statements reflect their perspectives:

I know it's tough, but we want you to stay safe. While this is not the way your school year should have ended, I look forward to celebrating with you as approach many new milestones.

You've got this!!

I would tell them that I continue to be here to support their educational needs.

I would want to remind them of their strengths, the contributions to the learning environment, and how they continue to impact our school community with their perseverance through the end of the year.

Elementary administrative personnel expressed a commitment to *celebrate* when it is safe to do so (n=11), *encouragement for their students* to continue to learn (n=7), and *confidence* that the students were ready (n=6). The following selected comments reflect their views:

We will celebrate when all of this is over.

Continue to learn and call us if you need assistance.

I would want to tell students that during this time, learning all they can about themselves, the value of relationships, and the privilege of freedom.

You are smart and intelligent, remember to try at all times.

You are ready to move on! We are sad that we didn't get to give you the traditional send off!

Middle school administrative personnel echoed elementary administrative personnel regarding a *celebration* when it is safe (n=4), *continuing to learn* (n=3), and *confidence* in the students' readiness (n=3) as expressed by the following statements:

We will make sure to come together to celebrate your school year!

To remember all that they've learned from me and continue to strive to reach their goals.

We are a better place because you were here, and you are prepared for the next step in your education because we not only built academics, but your ability to adapt and succeed.

Finally, high school personnel also indicated a desire to *celebrate* when it is safe (n=11) and a *confidence* that the students were ready (n=4), but their other top response varied from that of the other two levels. They made note that this was an *historical* or *unique event* (n=5) as evidenced by the following selected statements:

> We could never have anticipated this happening, but we will work to make sure you have memories for the end of the year. They may not be the ones that we had anticipated, but we will do something(s) to celebrate you.
>
> Your graduation class will be forever remembered about this event, and we are here to assist you as you move forward with your future plans.
>
> History has been made; they are prepared for the next level; college, life, military.

What Is Your Reaction to The Canceling of State Tests for This School Year?

The central office and all three levels of building administrators: elementary, middle, and high school responded that they *agreed* that the tests should be cancelled as their top theme; that they were *happy* the tests were cancelled as their second theme, and that they were in a state of *relief* as their third theme. Additionally, participants from all four groups furthered their comments suggesting a revamping of accountability, a concern for equity related to testing, or cancelling of standardized tests as illustrated by the following statements:

> Should probably be cancelled forever. (CO)
>
> In the best of times, testing can be stressful for students - right now our students and families are worried, afraid, financially unsure, and may have to deal with sickness or death. Worrying about testing would be a ridiculous stress to put on our students during this time. (CO)
>
> I truly believe we will look at testing differently moving forward. (CO)
>
> It is the proper move. Maybe this will be an opportunity to revamp the system of accountability and what it looks like. (E)
>
> Excitement. I hope this shows that students are more than tests and that the demonstration of learning can take more forms than a test they essentially proved very little about a student's ability to learn and be successful. (M)
>
> It needed to be cancelled. At least a quarter of my students do not have internet access and many of them are working or taking care of their siblings. It is not equitable to continue with state testing. (H)

How Do You See This Interruption Impacting Future Classes and Students?

From the central office respondents, the most prevalent theme was *learning gaps* (n=16), which included overall learning and among sub-groups, with associated equity concerns. This theme was followed by *concern for social emotional support* (n=5) and anticipated *change in instructional delivery* (n=5). Instructional change referenced not only changes in teacher delivery but also improved or increased online instruction. The following statements characterize the thoughts and feelings of this sample of school administrators during this COVID-19 experience:

> The closure of schools for the remainder of the year will require that we provide additional instruction in the coming school year to address "gaps in learning."
>
> A new way of delivering instruction and the need to address the equity concerns for all students and their families.
>
> We are also aware that some of our students will not come back to us as they were before this experience, and that we will need to be very aware of their mental and physical wellness upon return. I worry that this will add to the many things that many of our students worry about in day-to- day life. They are aware of so many scary things in the world, and I do think this weighs on them and shapes their decisions about life - now they will have one more horrible thing to worry about happening again. It will be part of our job to infuse joy, hope, goodness, and positivity in to their daily lives.

Elementary respondents also most frequently addressed *learning gaps* (n=26), closely followed by *equity* (n=13). Their third-highest theme was *social emotional support* (n=10) as indicated by the following selected statements from this sub-group:

> Academic gaps, inequities, and mental health.
>
> I am most concerned about the gaps which are forming emotionally, behaviorally, and academically for students.
>
> All students, regardless of how their school or system handled this, will have some type gaps in learning.

Middle school respondents identified *learning gaps* (n=10) most frequently. Their second most frequent theme addressed *changes in practice*, including more technology, opportunity to innovate, and change in instructional strategies in the classroom. The final theme was one of *confidence* (n=3), indicating that students were resilient and would be fine. Their views are captured by the following statements:

> We are preparing for a decline in academic achievement and how the beginning of school should look like when students return.
>
> It will be an opportunity for innovation among educators to determine what is needed next.
>
> I think we are going to be just fine. I think this experience will unite us in the education world.

We have been innovative in our approaches as a collective.

High school leaders responded similarly with their most frequent identified theme being *learning gaps* (n=17). *Change in instructional delivery and practice* was the second most frequently mentioned theme (n=6). Finally, *equity* (n=3), beyond learning gaps was noted. Accordingly, the following selected comments reflect the high school administrators' views:

Students will surely appreciate school more—the social and emotional support they get there.

There will be learning gaps that will exacerbate the gaps that already existed along lines of race, ethnicity, and poverty.

This will continue to impact underserved and marginalized groups. This interruption will affect us for years to come. We will need to get very creative to address the negative impact of school closing on students who have historically been underserved to begin with. This interruption also shines light on the growing educational (resources, technology, access) inequities between the "haves" and the "have nots."

This time has allowed me to challenge my teachers to be more performance based and standards based when creating lessons. These areas are so needed, in my opinion, and we are seeing students becoming more successful as they complete these critical thinking and analysis-based lessons. It is hard for the age old "sage on the stage" to continue when one is online thankfully.

WHAT IS YOUR OPINION OF HOW SCHOOL YEAR GRADES SHOULD BE FINALIZED IF STUDENTS DON'T RETURN TO SCHOOL?

The vast majority of leaders at all levels indicated that the *grades should not be negatively impacted* after the closing of schools. This was noted by central office (n=22), elementary (n=33), middle (n=13), and high school (n=15) leaders and is reflected in the following selected comments from this sample:

Grades will be given as of the last day of traditional schooling. Students will have to option to improve the grade. (CO)

Our students will not drop lower than what they had when they left. They do have the opportunity to make a higher grade based on meeting mastery for standards. (E)

I don't believe that we count the grades collected if they are going to have a negative impact on the student's overall grade. This is a new way of teaching for our teachers and learning for our students. They should not be punished for the lack of technology, internet, or lack of learning in this manner. (M)

In order to assess fairly, in a community where online access is limited and the ability to provide materials directly is limited, the expectation of continued learning without grading or recognizing effort for improvement seems to be the proper decision. (H)

However, the second and third most common themes identified from the central office sub-group of administrators were using the *Pass/Fail option* (n=6) and *concerns over equity* (n=3) as reinforced by the following comments:

The last quarter should be pass/fail. . . . No child should fail because they cannot access the work provided.

I don't believe that accessibility to internet, virtual classrooms should deter a student and preclude them from advancing.

But, at the elementary level, the second and third most common themes were *equity* (n=6) and the *grade should only improve* (n=5) as evidenced by these statements:

There is no way to collect grades and make it equitable for all.

Our students will not drop lower than what they had when they left. They do have the opportunity to make a higher grade based on meeting mastery for standards.

And, middle school leaders followed elementary leaders with their second theme of *equity* (n=3) tied with their third theme of *considering a pass/fail option* (n=3) as reflected in these statements from their sub-group:

They should not be punished for the lack of technology, internet, or lack of learning in this manner.

Students with an F will complete work to earn a D. Students with grades of an A-D can choose that as their final grade or choose a "P."

The second and third most frequently mentioned themes from high school leaders was that *students can only improve* (n=8), and the *pass/fail option* should be used (n=5) as the following comments from their sub-group members indicate:

Allow any work students complete to raise their grade, but it cannot lower their grade. Any work done during distance learning can help a student, but not hurt a student's grade.

Students that demonstrate mastery during distance learning can raise their grade.

Keep a pass/fail grading approach that is blended into the 4th marking period.

As We Capture This Moment in Time What Else Should We Record?

It is difficult to identify major themes from the variety of responses to this question, so the following are selected comments from each group that tell a story.

Central Office

We should record the amazing things people are doing in our communities to help others. It always amazes me that it takes horrible events for people to display their love, generosity, heroism, and strength. I wish these were things we witnessed on this scale daily, no matter what was going on in the world.

The positives of how Educational companies and educators in general have risen to the occasion and provided students with meaningful learning opportunities during this crisis.

The impact this has on the mental and emotional state of our students.

We should record the number of students that did not have access to all the opportunities that some children had. We have a long way to go when it comes to equity in education.

I think we should record how this stress is impacting families. We should look at which populations are being adversely affected.

The steep learning curve and adaptability of students and teachers and the support everyone is giving each other to get by.

We should record that we as educators have to be more proactive in our approach. It is time for education to evolve into the century in which we live.

Elementary

Expect the unexpected. You cannot plan for every situation that may occur, but be prepared to adjust and be flexible in difficult times. We will survive!

How underfunded our social services system may be when it comes to taking care of the poor.

I believe there has been an improved appreciation for teachers and the school community. . . . Some of the lowest paid employees in the district have had the most risk. For example, cafeteria workers, instructional assistants, and bus drivers are the ones still working out in public to get food to students.

We need to learn from this Pandemic as much as we can. It's not a matter of "if" but "when" the next one comes, will we be ready? Our way of life has forever been changed and impacted. Unprecedented, for sure!

Middle School

How school divisions handled the "caring for the Health and wellness of their staff" Are employees just numbers or are they people that may have emotional and social needs during this time just as much as the students we serve.

Solidarity and extensive efforts to meet inequitable access that some students faced

The sheer number of education professional professionals who have stepped up to do what's best for kids is inspiring!

This is uncharted for all, but we are in it together.

High School

The feeling. The pictures of the streets in our major cities being empty, but also how we have pulled together as communities and a nation. The generosity and kindness that we have seen displayed toward all communities. There are greater needs now. Not only will we need to recover from the impact on loss of life, but economically, how we will pull together to lift all of us up.

This time has opened the eyes of many to how woefully unprepared divisions and schools are to be equitable and equal during times of crisis or change when providing instruction and materials for all students in their community/state.

The students, staff, and community are learning empathy and resiliency. Physical distancing and social distancing are two different actions. Humans need social interaction. We are capable of keeping a physical distance but remaining socially interactive with technology.

Mental wellness and preparedness to endure such a tumultuous time must be considered, moving forward.

In life, things happen for a reason. Let us move onward and upward on the other side.

COMMON THEMES OF 2020

While the themes have been shared by group and by question, there were some overarching themes that were apparent from all participant categories. Those themes were the importance of family, the need for access to technology, the need to revisit the purpose and validity of standardized state testing, and equity for all students.

Importance of Family

The responses from the participants indicated that they were as worried about food for their students as they were about continued learning. They mentioned worry over the social emotional needs of the students and their parents. They further referenced concern for the family of educators with whom they worked. The following statements reinforce these concerns of the educational leaders who participated in this study:

> Making sure students' needs were met, including food, social & emotional needs, offering support.
> Making sure we have a means to get food and resources for our students.
> Reassuring/emotional support for teachers and students.
> The public health and safety of our school community. We then began to think about how we could provide some aspect of a continuity of learning.

Need for Access to Technology

Technology, while often available at school, failed to guarantee quality use for instruction. In some cases, the teachers were not prepared to teach effectively online. In other cases, the infrastructure and access to broadband internet in the homes of teachers and/or students was not assured. Accordingly, study sample representatives offered the following comments:

> We have many rural areas in our district and we are known for poor internet access, so we did not have a learn at home system in place for school closings.
> How do we provide a continuity of learning for students with no digital access?
> I believe my teachers will be more prepared to adapt their traditional classroom-based lessons to electronic formats.

Need to Revisit the Purpose and Validity of Standardized State Testing

A concern that continued to be expressed in a number of the responses from this study sample related to the value of standardized testing, both in relation to the instructional time lost to prepare, time devoted to taking the tests, and the time needed to remediate after taking the tests as well as in relationship to the potential inequity, as implied by the alignment of levels of poverty in the community and levels of academic performance on the tests. The following selected study sample comments express this concern about the value of testing:

I believe my teachers will be more prepared to adapt their traditional classroom-based lessons to electronic formats.

It is an opportunity to engage in 21st century skills and not "teach to the test." It is an opportunity to engage students in deeper learning and cross-curricular activities.

Equity for All Students

Equity was mentioned or referenced within the responses to standardized testing, to online learning, to first thoughts, and to future considerations. The concept permeated the study, and was woven in the themes of technology, family, and testing as illustrated by the following representative comments:

A new way of delivering instruction and the need to address the equity concerns for all students and their families.

There will be a gap instructionally, behaviorally, and emotionally for our students. It will be difficult and a little scary for them coming back. We need patience and consistency to help fill the gap.

We will need to get very creative to address the negative impact of school closing on students—who have historically been underserved to begin with. This interruption also shines light on the growing educational (resources, technology, access) inequities between the "haves" and the "have nots."

CONSULTING THE EXPERTS

As part of this study, a Post-Hoc Panel of experts with previous administrative pre-K–12 experience as well as university educational leadership professors, reviewed the findings and provided valuable analytical insights. The panel was asked to comment on the specific themes and overarching findings presented in the study. Experts also made comments on the immediate and long-term implications from the coronavirus and opportunities for change and reflection. The following are themes and noteworthy considerations shared by the panel of experts.

Social Emotional Learning

Consider the social emotional needs of learners first. Incorporate supports a student might need to be successful within the curriculum. Educational leaders, school staff, and "others designing interventions to improve achievement of disadvantaged students should address social-emotional competencies and classroom climate, especially teacher support of students" (Elias & Haynes,

2007, p. 474). Education first and foremost begins with students who are ready and willing to learn.

Collaboration

Teachers at the present time must accept students where they are, both academically and emotionally. In many cases that means getting students ready to learn before real learning can take place. This can no longer be solely the responsibility of the teacher. There should be a much more collaborative system and process for ensuring that all students are ready to learn.

The collaborative system may mean appropriately feeding everyone who needs food. It may mean health screenings prior to enrollment. It may mean social interventions and mental health services to accompany each learner's plan of study. Finally, it may mean an individualized educational plan, including transitional components, that will identify steps to prepare the student to become a productive member of society.

A process for assessing a student's readiness at the outset of schooling will be crucial to their success. "Social-emotional competence and social support have been hypothesized to have strong influences on academic trajectories during the critical period of academic skill acquisition" (Elias & Haynes, 2007, p. 474).

Parents and other key stakeholders also need to be in a cooperative venture with the school and the teacher to ensure students come to school prepared and ready to learn. Once students are in school, choosing teachers that care will be crucial to their success. Teachers have to be vested in each student's success.

Teachers must employ learning methodologies and instructional strategies that are engaging and motivating to students. COVID-19 has shined a spotlight on how fragile our students are and how important social interaction is to our students. Mental wellness is crucial in helping students be successful. "Strong school-community partnerships are essential for a world-class, 21st century education, and more and more communities across the country are creating such partnerships" (Roche & Strobach, 2019, Introduction).

Restructuring Education

There are many considerations related to restructuring the educational system based on the comments of this study's sample of school administrators. Several are articulated here for reader's consideration and reflection. The educational system, as it selects and utilizes teachers, needs to be revamped to mirror elements commonly found in other professions. Consideration should be given to creating tiers for teacher assignments and growth that could include apprenticeships and master teachers.

Master teachers might be able to match other tiered classroom teachers with students whose needs and skills are aligned based on performance and skill sets. There should be no longer a one size fits all model of education for students. Instead, like the technicians, nurses, and physicians in the medical field, it is proposed by this panel that statewide educational leaders and policymakers dramatically change the way teachers are ranked, organized, and paid.

In response to this recommendation, those who fund education will need to provide a pay scale comparable to that of other professions so the selection pool is wider and deeper. There is no question that there are quality teachers in the field now and that they make a difference in the lives of students. However, as shortages are faced in a variety of curricular areas, the need to attract additional teachers of quality is imperative.

With a lucrative pay scale, a more representative population of teachers, including more teachers of color and more males, would be encouraged to become members of the education community. Incentives would need to be created to attract and retain the best and the brightest among them.

Dilworth's research suggested, educational leaders need to "take a more central leadership role in collaborating with other stakeholders to recruit and retain a diverse teacher workforce, and advocate for state and federal policies that first recruit and then retain teachers who are diverse and highly qualified" (Dilworth & Coleman, 2014, p. iii).

The acknowledgment of emerging needs beyond academic needs also has to be up for discussion. There should be no silos between social services and schools. "Further research should take advantage of the full depth and complexity of the [emerging needs in a wholistic] approach, remain sensitive to the unique features of the [school] care context, and devote particular attention to identity mobilization and context change as key drivers of system transformation" (Kriendler, Dowd, Star, & Gottschalk, 2012, Abstract).

Schools should become the center of the community. Schools will be open all day every day throughout the calendar year, and they can host a variety of services all designed to support the student beyond academic knowledge. If we believe education is the great equalizer and we believe the way up for all is to acquire a great education, then school and the education of each individual is crucial to the future success of the individual, the community, and our country.

The concept of school as the center of the community will require creating and building partnerships with social service and health services to provide all necessary services for students. Community partnerships with local law enforcement need to be forged as well. This new structure will require

building relationships with parents and the community that work exception-
ally well in terms of student support and also work well so that all community
members are sufficiently sustained during a crisis.

Having a system of this nature would have made a significant difference
in the delivery of services and supports during the Coronavirus and also
might have mitigated the challenges faced by our summer of unrest. Bryan
and others have proposed "a model to help school counselors navigate the
process and principles of partnerships. They define partnerships; discuss
the principles of democratic collaboration, empowerment, social justice,
and strengths focus that should infuse partnerships; enumerate a partnership
process model; and discuss implications for practice and research" (Bryan &
Henry, 2012, abstract).

The newly created culture will encourage empathy and understanding
among all school stakeholders. "Students today must be prepared not only to
pass tests at school but also to pass the tests of life. Social-emotional competence and academic achievement are highly related, and effective schools
are focusing efforts on integrated, coordinated instruction in both areas to
maximize students' potential to succeed in school and throughout their lives"
(Zins & Elias, 2007, p. 233).

Equity

Schools are more than educational facilities; they are flagships for the community—meeting academic, nutritional, and social and emotional needs of
students and families. The research from this study clearly asserts that there
is progress to be made regarding equitable educational opportunity for all
students. In light of the coronavirus pandemic and sudden shift to distance
learning, school divisions in the United States were reminded of the stark
educational inequities that have plagued our education system throughout history.

Today, the need for all students to have internet access is crucial in ensuring that all students have equitable opportunities to engage in distance
learning. Government must provide the digital infrastructure to rural areas
to afford families the opportunity to access school resources. Internet access
in the twenty-first century is just as necessary and fundamental as electricity
was to the twentieth century.

No government entity would have considered electricity an unnecessary
luxury, and now the same sense of government support should be given to
universal internet access. Students need reliable internet access, computers
and other devices to access digital content, as schools must provide reliable
and accessible platforms for instruction.

Had universal access been the standard during the coronavirus, instruction could have continued equitably. It is far beyond the time to bridge these gaps in accessibility so students are not limited to educational opportunities by their address and zip code. The time is now to build and sustain schools that reflect the best our country has to offer. Our young people are our future and in these turbulent times, they need the best very educational opportunities to succeed. Our country and the world are depending on it!

On a further note related to equity, children from homes that are economically challenged come to school behind those who have been afforded greater exposure and opportunity. Providing preschool options for all students would allow those with limited opportunity to access learning and exposure earlier, bringing their fundamental knowledge in kindergarten more in line with their more privileged peers. The ability to start their academic journey without disadvantage would be equitable. Policy makers at the national, state, and local levels need to consider universal preschool as an investment in, and an equity opportunity for, our future.

School Culture

When faced with challenges, true leaders become *agents of change* and *models of fairness*. School administrators play a crucial role in the culture of the school and must lead by example. In times of crisis, school leaders need to be visible and clearly articulate the transformative vision for the organization. As in the case of the coronavirus, participants from the study shared that they first had to grapple with their own emotions and fears before being able to address the larger school community. Once the reality struck that schools were going to be closed for the remainder of the school year, administrators were charged with creating a vision for faculty, parents, students, and other stakeholders of what distance learning would look like in their school community.

A positive, resilient, and supportive school culture is essential in uncertain times. The school's leadership team has to pivot the organization's focus to restructure teaching and learning. This requires acknowledgement from school leaders that the situation will be challenging but that they will be there with you every step of the way.

It is also important for administrators to keenly listen to all stakeholders in the organization to find common concerns and opportunities for action in moving forward. When stakeholders feel heard and valued they often will provide extraordinary support for the new initiative. If a culture of accepting feedback and two-way communication has been created, then innovative suggestions and solutions may come from those same stakeholders the leaders are trying to support.

Utilization of Resources and Talent

In times of uncertainty and extraordinary challenges, true leaders are born. When school leaders begin to pivot the organizations vision, it takes masterful calculations to assess the strengths of individuals and team leaders and plan how to best utilize their talents. School leaders should inventory all resources, skill sets, and interests to position them where they will be most productive and supportive in accomplishing the new vision for the organization.

In this case of implementing distance learning (literally overnight), administrators first had to survey the infrastructure and technological platforms they could utilize for distance learning. Next, they had to consider the ready skill sets of their faculty and ability to transform their teaching pedagogy to online delivery. School divisions needed to ensure that teachers had access to computers and the internet to deliver online instruction from their homes. Once the technology was in place for teachers, administrators had to assess professional development needs of their teachers.

Teachers may need extensive professional development in utilizing research-based best practices for online learning. Teachers need to understand the framework for online learning and also how to develop creative learning opportunities for students. Lessons need to be engaging and highly motivating for students using digital resources and tools. Providing opportunities for asynchronous and synchronous lessons provides students with some level of choice in how they complete lessons but also gives them opportunities to engage with the teacher and classmates, which can also be motivating for students.

Providing synchronous and asynchronous access is also imperative to meet the internet access capabilities of students and families. Being agents of change requires teachers to be risk takers in trying new teaching pedagogy for teaching online. Principals need to encourage, support, and reward this type of innovative instruction. It is important for teachers to keep in mind the social and emotional needs of their students during these unprecedented times.

Teachers and school leaders should consider working closely with parents to see how the school community can best support them in learning and making sure that essential needs are being met for each student. Creating a team approach with parents to motivate students and hold them accountable for learning is essential for student growth and achievement. In order for the above to be effective, administrators need to *walk the walk* of what they are expecting their teachers to do.

Administrators need to be providing resources and materials, leading conversations with parents, and checking in with students to see how they are doing. For example, principals could join a synchronous class session to say hello to students and see how they are adjusting to online instruction, recognize and encourage teachers for their work, and ask for feedback on how this *new normal* is impacting their daily lives.

Data collected from these types of conversations and check-ins can assist administrators in developing next steps for continued growth and improvement in the delivery of online instruction and as well as social and emotional health of students.

It is important to note that many school divisions had touted their use of technology for instructional purposes and had provided one-to-one devices for their students. However, when they were faced with using those technologies successfully to continue instruction, they found themselves less prepared. Perhaps, the benefit of this crisis is the potential preparation for future challenges related to resources, training, and delivery.

Equity and Technology

There are many ways that equity needs to be addressed as it related to technology. Recent communication with Faust, former Director of Technology for Charlottesville Public Schools and recently appointed Executive Director of Technology for Chesapeake Public Schools, led to some insightful comments worthy of consideration and sharing. Faust indicated that there are a variety of considerations related to equity and they include the following:

- *Equity via access*—Access to hardware, access to software, access to internet-based resources, access anytime and anywhere (including, and/ or especially at home).
- *Equity via process*—Ensuring that teachers are integrating technology resources in an equitable and comparable way. Teachers vary in their usage and integration of technology depending on the rigor and level of the course of instruction.
- *Equity via technology selection*—This is an often-overlooked opportunity to enhance the equitable realities in education by choosing free and or very affordable, always available (cloud) solutions over more expensive solutions requiring a lot of support and with steep learning curves to begin using/creating with the tool. Is it possible to achieve the same result using an inexpensive device and cloud based free programs as the student could achieve with an expensive program and an expensive device?
- *Equity via accessibility*—Accessibility cannot be an afterthought. There are very real limitations to technology for students with sensory disabilities as well as English learners and students that are not yet reading or are limited in their ability to read text. Ensuring that platforms and

resources created are designed with universal accessibility as part of the design is crucial.

- *Equity via usability*—Usability is the number one factor in determining whether people will use a new technology and while this may be a bit of a qualitative measure, it is important. Users will tell you when something is usable and easy to understand.
- *Equity via compatibility*—Technology needs to work across screen sizes and various operating systems. It is important to avoid specific software or hardware requirements that limit the ease of implementation of a new technology solution across all users and all devices.
- *Equity via interoperability*—Technology tool adoption and integration must be done with attention given to how the new tools will work with existing systems and processes. When adopting a new technology solution, it is important to ask what other systems it will work with and how.
- *Equity via engagement*—because students are coming from various households each with parents/guardians that are likely to vary in their comfort with technology systems, it is imperative to provide training and support for parents via outreach and engagement to ensure that parents who may need additional support and training on supporting their child know where to find resources and who they can contact with questions.
- *Equity via instructional design*—Teachers must design the learning experiences with technology to be engaging and equitable. This may be the most obvious but also the most elusive as most teachers have had little or no formal training on designing technology-based learning content but have more recently found themselves required to do just that. (J. Faust, personal communication, June 22, 2020).

CHAPTER AUTHORS' FINAL THOUGHTS

The pandemic has inadvertently created an opportunity for real change in regards to teaching and, but will schools fully embrace the opportunities set before them? If nothing else, the Coronavirus has forced state and local agencies to recalibrate and reinvent teaching and learning when not in a traditional school setting. This may have provided opportunities for more open-ended instruction, more project-based learning, more student choice related to how they learn best, and advanced possibilities for excelling academically.

The hard questions are yet to be answered:

- When students transition back to the traditional school building, will teachers use this distance learning experience as a springboard for more innovative teaching and learning opportunities?

- Will teachers renew their commitment to the rigor and relevance growth model to ensure that learning is meaningful and motivating for students by engaging them in real-world problems and authentic learning experiences?
- Will national and state policy makers consider this opportunity to replace standardized testing with an accountability system that allows students to authentically demonstrate their learning through open-ended assessment throughout the school year?
- If we are utilizing authentic twenty-first-century assessments throughout the school year, can we discontinue high stakes testing that takes months of review to prepare for and months of remediation as a result of?
- Are we really measuring what we want students to learn?
- What are we really testing for anyway?
- Is testing a teacher accountability measure or student achievement measure, or a teaching to the test challenge?

The participants in this research study and panel of experts clearly articulated the desire for meaningful change in the assessing teaching and learning. The question that still remains is do educational leaders have the courage, tenacity, foresight, and ingenuity to create a system that provides all students with equitable authentic learning experiences, coupled with authentic student-centered assessments.

This would afford all children the opportunity to fully demonstrate scholarly knowledge, skills and dispositions in a manner that is constructive and productive. This would prepare students to be contributing members of society, taught to analyze situations, ask questions and critically think about situations before forming a solution instead of preparing the to fill in a bubble to answer a question with one correct answer.

However, knowing what was heard from educators and what has been seen in the United States compels one to consider the future of education differently. Beyond the pandemic, the United States has faced protests and demands for equal justice under the law.

It is the belief of the authors that the world has changed forever. It is hoped that the changes are positive and will address poverty, equity, and excellence. The future has always been dependent on the children, and it is no less so now.

> "Let us think of education as the means of developing our greatest abilities, because in each of us there is a private hope and dream which, fulfilled, can be translated into benefit for everyone and greater strength for our nation."
>
> —John F. Kennedy, thirty-fifth president

KEY PRAGMATIC LEADERSHIP
TAKEAWAYS FROM CHAPTER 1

* *Leaders must consider the needs of their stakeholders, internal and external, in order to provide the support that students need to be successful.* They should understand that adequate food is a fundamental need that must be fulfilled before learning can be optimized.
* *Leaders need to advocate for access and skills related to technology.* They must understand that both teachers and students need effective access for remote learning and the skills needed to effectively utilize the technology.
* *Leaders need to advocate for an accountability system that supports student learning.* They must actively encourage a revamping of accountability systems, so that learning is the constant and timing is flexible.
* *Leaders need to consider the filter of equity when addressing issues of importance.* They must consider what is needed for each child, teacher, and/or family, and respond based on that need, remembering the equal isn't always fair.

REFERENCES

Bryan, J., & Henry, L. A Model for Building School–Family–Community Partnerships: Principles and Process, Journal of Counseling & Development, September 12, 2012, https://doi.org/10.1002/j.1556-6676.2012.00052.x

Dilworth, M. E., Coleman, M. J. Time for a Change: Diversity in Teaching Revisited, NEA Association Report, 2014, URI http://hdl.handle.net/10919/84025

Faust, J. Personal communication, June 22, 2020.

Kreindler S. A., Dowd, D. A., Star, N.d., Gottschalk, T. Silos and Social Identity: The Social Identity Approach as a Framework for Understanding and Overcoming Divisions in Health Care. *Milbank Quarterly*, June 18, 2012. https://doi.org/10.1111/j.1468-0009.2012.00666.x

Roche, M. K., Strobach, K. V. Nine Elements of Effective School Community Partnerships to Address Student Mental Health, Physical Health, and Overall Wellness, *Coalition for Community Schools. 2019*, https://files.eric.ed.gov/fulltext/ED593295.pdf

Zins, J. E., & Elias, M. J. Social and Emotional Learning: Promoting the Development of All Students, *Journal of Educational and Psychological Consultation*, April 2007, 17 (2–3), pp. 233–255. DOI: 10.1080/10474410701413152

Chapter 2

A Practicing Superintendent's Experiences During a Global Crisis

Recommendations for Preparing for the Next One!

Jeffrey Robert Rabey

"The Chinese use two brush strokes to write the word 'crisis.' One brush stroke stands for danger, the other for opportunity. In a crisis, be aware of the danger—but recognize the opportunity."

—John F. Kennedy (1959)

The above citation resonated with this author and other school leaders as they reflected about the impact of the global pandemic crisis of 2020–21 and the leadership approaches employed by school district superintendents of schools. Kennedy's intent in delivering the above quote was to promote perseverance through the multitude of crises that were unfolding all over the world at that time.

This chapter is written through the experiential lens of a practicing New York suburban superintendent named Dr. Jack Robbins (pseudonym), who has been a superintendent of schools for over fifteen years and is very well known to the authors of this book. It is the intent of the author that readers will reflect upon the above words of Senator Kennedy and see how they resonate at present time given the harsh global pandemic threats and the need for educational leaders to enthusiastically and creatively persevere during crises.

In this chapter, the author presents a historical perspective about the initial phases of the COVID-19 crisis and specifically illustrates the reactions of Jack Robbins and his school superintendent colleagues as they confronted an unexpected global crisis and successfully managed the people, things, and ideas associated with their school systems.

Through refencing real historical events regarding COVID-19 in New York and this school superintendent's direct responses to them as the leader of the Dutchmill Central School District, the pseudonym given to the real school district of this case study, readers are introduced to astute micro-context leadership approaches and specific models for education crisis management. The articulated strategies and examples provided may be used to deal with any unexpected micro-context crises which are often exacerbated by macro-level procedural inconsistencies.

An analysis of Dr. Robbins' real-world reactions to official communications highlighted below substantiate the significance of effective crisis leadership based on unbridled persistence, adaptable creativity, focused empowerment, uninhibited commitment, authentic relationships, intensive caring, and diverse communications to with and for all stakeholders.

INITIAL COVID-19 PANDEMIC TIMELINE

Pre-Shut Down: Week 0 thru Week 8

On or about January 17, 2020, the first two cases of COVID-19 were identified within the United States. But, on March 1, 2020, the first coronavirus case was confirmed in New York. Then two days later, after two confirmed cases within New York State, Governor Andrew Cuomo signed a $40 million emergency management authorization for New York's coronavirus response, giving him broad powers to issue directives during the looming pandemic.

On March 7, 2020, with his first official COVID-19-related executive order, Governor Cuomo declares a State of Emergency. On March 9, 2020, the New York State Department of Health and the New York State Education Department released a joint memo to school districts and health department officials. The memo was titled, *School (PreK-12) Guidance: COVID-19* (Zucker & Tahoe, 2020).

The memo addressed key areas related to the management of the people, things, and ideas of schools such as Travel-Related Considerations for Schools; Guidance for Schools to Prepare for COVID-19; Review, Update, and Implement Emergency Plans; Non-pharmaceutical Interventions; Guidance for Schools with Identified Cases of COVID-19 in Their Community;

Communication; Other Student Needs During School Closure; and Frequently Asked School and COVID-19 Questions and Answers.

School superintendents began to meet regionally and formulate a consistent set of procedures and communication plans to their stakeholders. Superintendents looked to their county health departments to provide clear guidance on immediate cancellations of traveling outside of the area and holding large events (awards ceremonies, musicals, and sporting events).

On March 11, 2020, with 216 confirmed cases in New York state, the governor announced that the State University of New York and the City University of New York institutions would begin distance learning for the remainder of the spring 2020 semester.

Subsequently, local school superintendents began to communicate with each other and meet with their faculty and staff to address some of the salient issues raised by the COVID-19 guidance provided by the New York State Department of Health and the State Education Departments:

1. The twenty-four-hour closure of a school when a student or staff member was diagnosed with the virus and how to then evaluate next steps.
2. Superintendents were not expected to make decisions about closing their district; this was not like a snow day. They were to be advised by the Department of Health and the State Education Department.
3. Regionally, school districts were advised by the County Departments of Health, to suspend all school related travel outside of their areas. This included field trips, athletic competitions, and conferences.
4. School districts were also advised by the Departments of Health and County Executives, until further notice, to suspend all public gatherings of fifty or more people. This included musicals, various celebrations and upcoming sporting events.
5. Moving forward, superintendents began to evaluate their district's ability to support the **Continuity of Instruction** through remote learning, as they were unsure of when schools would be closed down. They prepared for all scenarios, as it could have been as complex as direct instructional delivery via distance learning platforms or as simplistic as supplemental material support, in order to avoid any regression. They needed to be prepared for as little as a two-week dismissal of students to as long as six weeks or more.

As events began to accelerate, Superintendent Jack Robbins sent the following email to his faculty and staff on Friday, March 13, 2020:

Good Morning,

In light of the District-wide meetings that were held yesterday, the rolling emergency school closures in other states and to prepare for the worst case scenario; I am currently requesting that at all teachers send students home with materials essential (e.g. text books, workbooks, etc.) for continuous learning TODAY. I realize that this is a short time frame, but I am asking our TOSAs and principals to set aside other tasks for the time being and identify and communicate to our teachers what should be included in the list of "essential materials."

Please note: We have not been instructed to close schools at this point in time. This is a precautionary measure being taken for the benefit of our students in the event that we are instructed to close schools.

I am so proud of this faculty and staff and so appreciative to all of you for pulling together to help navigate through this fluid and unprecedented situation. Our students and our extended school-community are very fortunate to have you! Please let me know if you should have any questions or additional thoughts.

Stay safe!

Jack

Shut Down: Week 9 thru Week 23

On Sunday, March 15, 2020, school closings began in New York City, Westchester, Nassau, and Suffolk counties, and Superintendent Robbins sent the following email to his Board of Education:

Good Morning,

As anticipated. The County Executive announced a State of Emergency effective noon today. We have been in constant contact with his office over the past two days. We are meeting with him and the DOH at 4pm today at BOCES. As stated, we will be closed beginning tomorrow. The Administrative Team will be meeting at 9am to identify any gaps in our plans to best serve our students and our community at large during the closure. We do have a plan to feed our students and will be releasing that to the community tomorrow. Our waiver to provide meals to our students was approved by NYSED this morning.

I will provide you an update tomorrow morning.

Jack

This was the subsequent message sent to his school community:

In accordance with the County Executive's recommendation that people avoid large gatherings of more than 50 people, and in light of the declaration of multiple States of Emergency, all County school districts will be closed until April 20, 2020. During the week of the April 13th we will determine if the length of closure will need to be extended.

Please continue to check our website for updates.

Then on Monday, March 16, 2020, Governor Cuomo issued an executive order closing all schools across the state. Also, the governor suspended the 180-day instructional requirement for schools and instructed school districts to develop a plan for continuity of instruction, along with a meal plan, and childcare for the essential workforce.

On March 17, 2020, the New York State Education Department issued a memo on Additional Guidance on Statewide School Closures Due to Novel Coronavirus (COVID-19) Outbreak in New York State identifying that schools should be implementing response plans and have established mechanisms for ongoing communications with staff, students, families, and communities during the time of closure.

In addition, it addressed the directive for school districts to establish a COVID-19 closure plan for alternative instructional options (electronic and non-electronic), distribution and availability of meals, and child care, with an emphasis on serving children of parents in the health care profession or first responders who are crucial to the response effort. These plans needed to be submitted to the State Education Department no later than by 5:00 p.m. on Thursday, March 19, 2020 (Tahoe, 2020).

On March 23, 2020, the following message was relayed to Dutchmill School-Community by Superintendent Robbins:

Good Morning,

This message is from Dr. Robbins and the Dutchmill Central School District. Due to the recent directive from the Governor that 100% of non-essential workers must stay home, the main offices in all of the school buildings within Dutchmill Schools will be closed until further notice. The District will still be providing the essential services of meals, child care for the essential work force and the continuity of instruction. Information on all three of these essential services can be found on our website. If you have any questions or have any needs, please call the respective offices and someone will be sure to call you back. The phone numbers for all offices can be found on our website at www .depewschools.org. Please continue to regularly check our website for updates on all of our available resources during this health emergency.

Stay Safe.

On March 27, 2020, Cuomo extended the statewide school closures by an additional two weeks. The next day, he postponed the school board elections and budget votes until at least June 1, 2020.

On March 30, 2020, via an email from the New York State Education Department, all school districts were notified that they, " . . . must continue to provide remote instruction for students, meals for students, and child care for essential workers every weekday between April 1, 2020 and April 14,

2020, even if the district is scheduled to be on spring break during that time."
(NYSEDP12, Personal communication, March 30, 2020)

As a result of an ever-evolving set of circumstances and attempting to
ensure that, as an organization, they were addressing all of the concerns that
they needed to, Dr. Robbins conducted an online survey via ThoughtExchange.

Per their website ThoughtExchange.com, the surveying process utilized in
receiving feedback is "To keep pace with digital transformation, leaders of all
types need to evolve how they lead: from loud leadership to crowd leadership.
Crowd leaders who activate everyone to solve challenges together outperform
loud leaders who make decisions and then influence people. The wisdom of
crowds is powerful and scalable" (ThoughtExchange.com, 2020).

In order to solicit constructive feedback, the following message was sent
out to the faculty and staff by Dr. Robbins, via an email:

> Good Morning,
> We now have found ourselves looking at a longer-term closure in response
> to the COVID-19 crisis. As we continue to navigate this transition, it's more
> important than ever that we stay connected. There are many moving pieces right
> now. We are considering how to run interactive remote classes and meetings,
> how to keep our staff safe, and how to set you and students up for success dur-
> ing this challenging and uncertain time. I'm sure many of you have questions
> and ideas that you want to share, and we want to make sure we're hearing what
> everyone has to say. I firmly believe we are smarter and better together and I am
> asking you for five minutes today and another five minutes tomorrow to help
> us plan for this new way of working. Please share your thoughts and questions.
> Please also come back to this link sometime tomorrow, Saturday and Sunday, in
> order to star the thoughts shared. We will use the collective knowledge of our
> staff to help our planning efforts around how we stay connected and productive
> as a team. This exchange will be open until Sunday, April 5th. I thank you in
> advance for your willingness to participate in this exchange.
> Here is the question: As we continue to navigate through the impact of the
> COVID-19 crisis, what are the most important things that we should be consid-
> ering, in order to keep everyone (students, parents and teachers) connected and
> productive, as we look at a longer-term closure?

According to Superintendent Robbins, the responses were overwhelming,
with 193 participants and 234 different thoughts; major themes surfaced
as a result:

- Ability to reach students/maintain engagement
- Communication
- Distance learning practices/processes
- Impact on curriculum/grading/next year

- Issues with online tools/access to devices
- Mental health and well being
- Reasonable and consistent academic expectations
- Support for students/families

As a result of the analysis of the survey and the need to share the feedback with the faculty so that collectively they could refine their response and support in the wake of the closure, the following communication was sent:

Good Morning Dutchmill Family,

As a follow up to the recent ThoughtExchange and specifically some concerns around communicating to our students, I would like to offer you some clarity and rationale for the direction that the District, has taken on communicating with our students, "Teachers are expected to maintain a log of their communication efforts for students that **have not** engaged in online learning. Each building principal is designing what this tool will be. *We must be overt in our outreach to families of students not participating.* Minimally each teacher must call each family twice and send email correspondence as well to identify reasons for lack of engagement." To further clarify, "Phone calls only need to be made to parents of students that have not participated at all and if there is contact on the first attempt, a second phone call does not need to be made." Furthermore, each teacher of the student does not need to call, this can be divided up amongst the various grade levels or teams of teachers. This will be explained in further detail in upcoming ILT, department and grade levels meetings later this week.

As you are aware, in order to receive constructive feedback, on the crisis and the closure, from all faculty and staff, the district conducted a ThoughtExchange back on April 2nd and the major themes were as follows:

- Ability to Reach Students/Maintain Engagement
- Communication
- Distance Learning Practices/Processes
- Impact on Curriculum/Grading/Next Year
- Issues with Online Tools/Access to Devices
- Mental Health and Well Being
- Reasonable & Consistent Academic Expectations
- Support for Students/Families

As you can clearly see, several key themes are around communicating with our students and their well-being! Therefore, this two-way communication expectation is imperative and supports what we are all collectively thinking and reflecting upon, when we are considering our students. We understand that when we call our students and/or their parents we will not have all of the answers to their questions and we can simply state, "We can get that information for you" or "We will have someone call you" or "More details about that will be coming out shortly." Furthermore, please know that at any time, just like when we are in session, when you are communicating with a student and/or a parent and if there appears to be an emotional / hardship / neglectful situation that becomes apparent, please refer that student/parent to their assigned school counselor. The school counselor can then reach out to that family as soon as possible.

Finally, to further clarify, two-way communication does **NOT** mean that a parent simply picked up their child's learning packet or that the student has received emails from their teacher or that assignments have been shared via Remind. Two-way communication means that there has indeed been a back and forth communication (emails, phone calls, submitted assignments with teacher feedback), that we know that your student is connected and engaged or at the very least okay!

I hope this goes a long way at clearing up any misinterpretation about the district's expectation for communicating with our students. Next Monday (4/20), we are also planning to begin weekly check-ins on each student, by having our secretarial staff call every family's home, in order to determine if they are in need of anything. We will maintain a spreadsheet database and direct any of their needs to the appropriate resources, both in district and out of district.

As always, if you have any questions, concerns or are in need of further clarification, please feel free to contact us.

Be Safe and Stay Healthy!

Jack

Then on April 6, 2020, Governor Cuomo extended NY on PAUSE closures by two weeks and ordered schools and nonessential businesses closed through April 29, 2020. The next day, the state's education department provided clear guidance on the cancelation of the end of the year's Regents Exams. As a result, the following communications were delivered by Dr. Robbins to his faculty and staff and the entire Dutchmill school-community:

Good Afternoon,

As I send this important email update, I hope everyone is healthy and staying safe. Below is a detailed communication on how the District will be moving forward with our extended closure. I also attached a copy of the Community Letter that is being made available to parents today on our Website.

Based upon Governor Cuomo's recent executive orders and the guidance set forth by the New York State Education Department, the Dutchmill Central School District will remain closed through April 29, 2020 due to COVID-19 crisis.

The Governor's Executive Order also mandates that schools must continue to provide remote instruction for students every weekday, even during the dates schools were scheduled to be on spring break. Failure to provide continued instruction and other identified services could result in a loss of state school aid. The New York State Education Department confirmed that instruction should also be in effect on Friday, April 10th, which normally would be a non-attendance day for the Good Friday religious holiday. Dutchmill teachers will continue the continuity of instruction through April 29th and beyond, should the governor extend school closing beyond this date.

Yesterday, April 7, 2020, the Education Department supplied school districts with the necessary guidance on the cancelation of the Regents exams. This specifically applies to students who, during the June 2020 examination period would have taken one or more Regents examinations. These students will be exempt from passing the Regents assessments in order to be issued a diploma in the future. Our building principals and school counselors will be sending detailed information to all grade 6–12 students and parents on the specific details of this most recent development.

The Education Department also clarified how students will earn course credit for their courses this year to count toward the twenty-two (22) credits required for graduation. They have explained that as long as the student has met the standards assessed in the provided coursework, the student should be granted the diploma credit. It was further explained that with distance and online learning methods being utilized during this extended school closure, the **priority for the instruction should be that which best prepares students to meet the learning outcomes for the course and prepare for the culminating examination/project.**

Although these most recent developments regarding Regents Exams and course credit are not applicable to our elementary and most of our middle-level students, collectively we still need to be committed to the concept of continuity of learning for these children, in order to reduce the effect of regression of learning. With that in mind, as the length of our closure persists, we must continue to review and enhance our academic and social/emotional offerings to our students. We understand that the sudden transition to distance learning has been challenging for all of you. We continue to examine all avenues that provide comprehensive educational services to each student every day. To that effect, please review an overview of the next phase of our learning plan below:

Our goal is to continue to provide quality educational interactions through Schoology and a variety of other online platforms throughout the emergency closure. While each classroom teacher might approach their distance learning instruction differently, the goal for the entire District remains the same, to help students achieve the learning standards for each course. To that end, please find the highlights to the district's plan:

- Teachers will continue to work across grade levels to ensure the continuation of a full roll-out of new, comprehensive online learning activities through April 29th and beyond if needed.
- Effective April 20th K-2 instruction will move on-line and away from instructional packets.
- The Third and Fourth Marking Periods for MS/HS and Second and Third trimesters for Cayuga will be blended and ultimately be dependent on the length of the closure.

- If students had any incomplete work prior to our closure on March 13, 2020, give them EVERY opportunity to make up this work.
- Students will only be receiving feedback (Exceeds Expectations, Meets Expectations or Incomplete) for their assigned work during the emergency closure and NOT a grade that would count toward a final average in their course. *The exception to this rule is for High School Advanced Studies Courses designed to receive College Credit (For Example: Advanced Studies Anatomy and Physiology, Advanced Studies Game Coding, etc.).
- Averages for all courses in grades 6–12 for the time period we are closed will be as follows:
  - EE: Exceeds expectations
  - ME: Meets expectations
  - *I: Incomplete*
- Grade 6–12 end of year projects (not final exams) will be discussed in future communication, should we remain closed through the end of the school year.
- As we continue through the emergency closure; Instructional Assignments and Activities are to be provided on a weekly basis in Schoology and/or on the district website: www.dutchmillschools.org
- These guidelines are recommended as the base standard for student engagement in their learning:
  - A minimum of ten (10) hours per week of online instruction and guided learning activities;
  - Two (2) hours minimum of online learning per day is suggested, but additional time on task instruction might be necessary and is encouraged for Middle and High School students.
  - *Students are encouraged to exercise each day, take brain breaks, and maintain healthy living activities*
- A weekly log of instruction needs to be maintained by each teacher. If you are using Schoology, this will be identified through various analytic reports.
- A template will need to be maintained and submitted to each principal from any teacher not using Schoology to deliver their instruction. This will be provided to you by your building principal.
- Teachers are expected to maintain a log of their communication efforts for students that have not engaged in online learning. Each building principal is designing what this tool will be. We must be overt in our outreach to families of students not participating. Minimally each teacher must call each family twice and send email correspondence as well to identify reasons for lack of engagement.

The circumstances around this continued public health challenge seem to change rapidly. We will continue to take action according to those circumstances, with the guidance of public health officials, the Governor's Office and the State Education Department, in an effort to promote the health and safety of our Dutchmill Family. Thank you for your unwavering commitment to your students and willingness to go above and beyond to make remote instruction work. Each of you are finding new and innovative ways to connect with students and to share messages of care, concern, and support. This is what makes the Dutchmill Family second to none. We are especially proud of re-energized partnerships between our teachers, staff, students, and parents, as we work through these challenges together.

Stay safe and be well,
Jack

On April 16, 2020, the continuation of school closures was extended through May 15, 2020, amid signs of the rate of hospitalizations slowly declining. As a way to promote further communications and connections with their families through the extended closure, the following protocol was designed and several faculty and staff members participated; from the administrative team, the secretarial pool and a group of exploratory teachers:

Good Morning Team,

I hope everyone is healthy and safe!

On Monday April 20th the District will begin making weekly phone call check-ins with our families. All of us on this email group are assigned families and will be making calls. We created the attached shared Google Sheet to facilitate this endeavor. You will just need to find your tab with your last name. Some of us may have more than one tab/families after Monday, as I am awaiting to assign some others to help us out in this initiative. If you end up getting more assignments, I will email you after Monday. You DO NOT have to call all of your families on Monday. You can divide the families up over the week, so that you might only have to call 5 to 7 a day. One important note, you may notice that some of the families on your sheet may be highlighted. This is due to the fact that they are already being contacted by our ELL staff, due to a language barrier and you will **not** have to call them.

You can record any important information from your conversations right in the Google Sheet. If after repeated attempts you cannot make a connection with any of your families, we will then be making welfare checks to verify phone numbers/email and to see if there are any services that the family may need. Attached to this email is the link to the Google Sheet and the Script and Procedures/Resources to use when making your calls.

If you have any questions, please let me know.

Stay Safe and Healthy!
Jack

Dr. Robbins shared the following procedures and script with the team conducting the weekly check-ins with the families:

DCSD COVID-19 Weekly Family Check-in Procedure

What are we doing?

We are asking that the assigned staff participate in weekly check in phone calls to families of our Dutchmill students beginning the week of April 20, 2020.

What will this sound like?

Here is a sample of what a check in call might sound like:
"Hello. My name is . . . I am calling on behalf of Dutchmill Schools to see how your child/children are doing. Do you need anything? Are the children able to access the instructional materials that have been assigned to them? Would you mind if I call and check in with you on a weekly basis?"

If there is no answer . . . please leave a message if you are able "Sorry I missed you. My name is . . . I am calling on behalf of Dutchmill Schools to see how your child/children are doing. We want to make sure the children are able to access the instructional materials that have been assigned to them? If you need support please let the building main office know how we can help. Here is my office phone and/or email address."

If calling from home or your personal cell phone dial *67 prior to the phone number. This will block caller id.

How are we doing this?

- We divided all of the families within the district by the staff involved in the Check-in phone calls and created a Google Sheet.
- There is a column labeled "Conversation Log," please document any important notes here; such as, "No answer, left message," "Family doesn't want to be contacted each week and will call if they need anything," "Have difficulty logging into Schoology and referred to Joe D'Amato," "Family needed information on how to get meals for the children." These are just some of the examples of the communications that you may choose to document.
- We will all have access to this living document and will be able to access it at any time, if and when there are any questions about the needs of a particular family throughout the continuing closure.
- Currently there are three columns labeled by week. We will continue to add weeks as needed.
- You do not need to call all families on the Monday of the week, you can stagger your calls throughout the week.

- If a parent or caregiver asks a question you cannot answer or has a need you cannot respond to, please take their information down and let the appropriate person know via email or phone. If you are uncertain where to direct a need, the following may help: (Actual school phone numbers not included in this chapter, template only)
  - Food and Nutrition:
  - *Mental Health and Well Being:*
    - Kindergarten and Grade 1:
    - Grade 2 and Grade 3:
    - Grade 4 and Grade 5:
    - Grade 6 and Middle School Special Education: Grade 7 and Grade 8:
    - Grades 9 thru 11 (A thru I) and Grade 12 (A thru G:
    - Grades 9 thru 11 (J thru N) and Grade 12 (H-O:
    - Grades 9 thru 11 (O thru Z) and Grade 12 (P thru Y:
    Grade 7 thru 12 Resiliency Counselor:
  - Special Education:
  - Elementary Instructional Questions:
  - Middle School Instructional Questions:
  - High School Instructional Questions:
  - Technology Questions:
  - Other Areas will be added as we learn what families need

Why are we doing this?

The goal is that each family in our Dutchmill School-Community gets at least one phone call a week from school personnel during these extraordinary times. It is one way for us to remain connected and assist where needed.

After hearing mostly from parents during the initiation of the weekly phone call check-ins, it was now time to reach out to sixth- through twelfth-grade students, in order to receive feedback; therefore, on April 21, 2020, the following invite to a ThoughtExchange survey was sent to students:

Good Morning Dutchmill Students,

I would like to take this opportunity to let you know that all of us at Dutchmill miss each and every one of you! We know that this closure has been hard on all of you and you need to know that we will continue to support you, as best as we can, by providing the essential services of continuity of learning, meals and child care for the children of essential workers.

At this point we would like to hear more from you and have you assist us in refining and enhancing our support. Please participate by answering the following question: **As a student, what are your thoughts and questions about the**

continued school closure due to the COVID-19 crisis, and how can we best support you?

You can join this conversation today and share your thoughts and questions by simply going to this link: https://my.thoughtexchange.com and the ThoughtExchange. Please also come back to this link sometime over the next few days and star the other thoughts shared by your fellow students.

We will use the results of this exchange to refine and enhance our support for you. This exchange will be open until Sunday, April 26th.

Quick Tips:

- This exchange is confidential. Your thoughts will be shared, but not your identity.
- Please be polite and respectful as you share and rate thoughts.
- If you see a thought that is rude, hurtful or identifies a person or group, you can report it by clicking in the upper right corner of the thought.
- You do not need to rate all thoughts in this exchange.It is appreciated and recommended to rate around 30 over the time the exchange is open.

For up to date information on the COVID-19 School Closure and available resources, please visit www.dutchmillschools.org.

Thank you for participating in this important conversation and we hope to see you very soon!

Dr. Robbins

This ThoughtExchange survey solicited 131 student responses with 108 different thoughts. The four major themes from these thoughts were: (1) Academics and Achievement, (2) End of the Year Activities (graduation, prom, etc.), (3) Social and Emotional Needs, and (4) Unanswered Questions. The following are the actual top five student thoughts collected for each theme:

1. Theme of Academics and Achievement (students shared the following):

This online learning can be difficult at times. It's hard to get some assignments done due to internet.

This COVID-19 crisis is stressful and having hours of schoolwork to do everyday is not helping and almost everyone I know is behind and struggling. This is important because most of us aren't learning we are just trying to pass and catch up because we are all stressed out.

There is too much homework and it makes me stressed most of the day. I each day I find myself doing homework for 7–8 hours maybe more maybe less. I'm also doing homework for classes I don't usually have to which adds on.

I am more of a person who likes routine, such as going to school every weekday. To me I find it hard to adjust to doing schoolwork online. I prefer listening to a teacher talk than to work online.

It's been hard and stressful because I don't think I'm getting taught I think I'm just doing work and I'm not really learning anything.

2. End of the Year Activities (graduation, prom, etc.) (students shared the following):

I would rather have graduation pushed back than not happen I would rather wait to walk the stage than to graduate high school not doing it.

Prom! Do not cancel prom. Reschedule it.

I just want to know if we are cancelling things or if we are pushing this to the summer. The big thing like graduation and prom. Also are local exams cancelled I know regents are cancelled and AP are online, but what about local exams.

If extracurricular activities were to be cancelled, such as sports, prom, follies, graduation etc. Is there a chance to schedule it over the summer? All of my fellow senior classmates feel they deserve the same recognition as the rest of the senior classes. We r willing to push back as far as needed.

Also, I know I'm not a senior but you should still have graduation because it's a big day for them. Don't take that away from them. Is the way we are getting graded going to affect my chances of applying for NHS as a junior?

3. Social and Emotional Needs (students shared the following):

The continued school closure is very difficult. I'm worried about the work and how teachers will be doing their "finals." It's difficult we are trying to learn from them but we are also on our own. ***(This was the number one rated thought in the survey.)**

I miss being at school. It is hard to focus on work at home and easier at school. It's also stressful having many things to get done by the end of the week.

I think it's awesome that staff at Dutchmill are helping with meals and child care. There's people in Dutchmill that may not be able to afford a Meal, some people have no one to watch there kid(s). This little effort will help many people

It's very difficult not seeing friends. As a person, I need to physically see and interact with people and friends that aren't in my house. That's pretty much impossible and its hitting hard.

Teachers are giving us a ridiculous amount of work that is causing me more stress than when I was in school. I think mental health is important during these times and I am doing so much work that I don't have time to focus on that.

4. Unanswered Questions (students shared the following):

When are we going to go back to school? I like learning at school better than what we are doing now.

When will Dutchmill announce that it is cancelling school for the rest of the year? I believe that school should be cancelled for the rest of the year, too much risk staying open.

I believe that it would be irresponsible if we were to open up school for the rest of the year. There would also be no point, as we don't have regents. It's important because you are possibly risking the health of your students. How do you know you actually rid the school of any possible illness?

What's going to happen to the 3 months of education we missed?

Everything is fine with me. I think I'm okay with the work being sent out. My question is, the school closure keeps on being extended, do you think we'll ever come back? How are the exams going to be changed?

As the administrative team evaluated each of the student responses, they shared the results with the faculty. They began to develop a response plan in order to provide more detailed information and support to their students through their online classes, mass emails, virtual class meetings, and direct phone calls. This assisted their students tremendously, as it reduced the level of anxiety and allowed them to refocus for the remainder of their remote learning experiences.

Then, as most school leaders anticipated, on Friday, May 1, 2020, Governor Andrew Cuomo announced that school buildings would remain closed through the end of the current 2019–2020 academic year. The governor's executive order did not have a specific end of year date, therefore, districts had the flexibility to modify calendars to avoid contractual complications. In the Dutchmill Central School System, the administration focused on ending their remote instruction after 180 instructional days were reached, which occurred on Thursday, June 11, 2020.

According to Dr. Robbins, they also focused on the teachers' collective bargaining agreement and the fact that they are obligated to 186 days. Therefore, the 2019–2020 academic year ended for teachers on Thursday, June 18, 2020.

The district sent out the following message about the end of the school year to the school-community:

Good Morning,

Thursday, June 11th will be the last day of school for all. Here are some important end of year dates and plans:

Friday, May 22 will become a day of remote learning. Directives from the state say students and staff will be required to learn and work on this previously scheduled break. On Thursday, May 21st, the meal program will distribute meals for Friday, May 22nd and Monday, May 25th (Memorial Day).

Monday, May 25 will remain as a Holiday for Memorial Day for both staff and students.

Plans will be communicated about collecting and returning personal belongings from school and returning school property.

Thursday, June 18th will be the last day for Teachers.

Friday, June 26 will be the last day of meal distributions and essential workforce child care.

Please continue to check the District Website for updates.

Stay Safe.

Dr. Robbins

On May 11, 2020, the New York State Education Department issued a memo to all school districts regarding "Supporting Students and Families Disconnected from School" (DeCataldo, 2020). The memo recognized all of the efforts, but drew attention to those families that were still disconnected from their schools.

The Dutchmill administrative team reviewed the various resources provided within the memo and felt confident that they were able to address most vulnerable families in the school district. Even if they could not connect with a family through electronic means or even a phone call, they sent their school resource officer to conduct a "well visit" and to reestablish a connection with that family.

In addition to the executive order about the end of the school year, the governor also modified the rules under which school districts are to conduct the 2020 annual meeting for the election of school board members and budget votes. The statewide uniform voting date was moved from May 19, 2020, to June 9, 2020. The manner for providing public notice of the annual meeting remained unchanged, except that the number of required publications was reduced from four to two.

The first notice needed to be sent to school district residents no later than twenty-eight days before the election, and must include notice for an adjourned budget hearing. School districts needed to send out postcard notices, which detailed the date of the election, date of the budget hearing, and a definition of a qualified voter. The annual meeting for the election of school board members and budget votes would take place remotely and qualified voters would vote only via absentee ballot.

School district officials needed to send out an absentee ballot to all qualified voters, with a postage paid return envelope for any election held on or
before June 30, 2020. School districts needed to submit their report card to
the State Education Department no later than May 22, 2020 (eighteen days
prior to June 9, 2020).

The governor's order also waived the minimum threshold number of signatures required for individuals to be placed on the ballot, except that they
must meet all other requirements, including applicable residency and age.
Candidates would be listed on the ballot alphabetically.

This last-minute pivot on the budget vote and board of education elections was met with a tremendous amount of disappointment and frustration
from school leaders. This adjusted process contained numerous hazards that
could be potentially devastating to schools. First, the timelines were difficult
to meet, as some schools had adopted budgets by their boards of education
already and some did not. Secondly, anyone could just deem themselves a
board of education candidate without having to collect any signatures from
their school community.

Finally, and most concerning, a ballot needed to be sent to every registered
voter within a school district. During the past ten years in the Dutchmill
Central School District, there has been an average of 667 voters who came to
the polls to cast their ballots with a high of 954 voters in 2011 and a low of
338 voters in 2019. With the new voting expectations, school district officials
in Dutchmill had to mail out almost eleven thousand absentee ballots to their
school community. As of Friday, June 5, 2020, only a few days away from the
new vote day, they received over 1,500 absentee ballots back from the voters.

This spike in votes was a similar trend in surrounding districts as well. This
development was very concerning as schools were closed since March, the
economy was struggling, and voters were feeling disenfranchised. The passing rates for school budgets were at all time low, with many school budgets
barely passing. The financial outlook for schools was bleak and the unknowns
were vast, as school leaders headed into the summer 2020, hoping for some
level of emergency federal stimulus targeted for schools.

THE COVID-19 CRISIS IN REVIEW

In order to be able to serve the children and families within their
school community, the Dutchmill Central School District administration
under the leadership of Superintendent Robbins engaged in emergency planning and deploying the necessary resources where they were needed. Since
March 16, 2020, their responses have significantly evolved through the following activities:

- Their Food Service Department immediately began offering breakfasts and lunches to district students, and as of Friday, June 5, 2020, they served over seventy thousand meals and Superintendent Robbins was there every single day to serve the community;
- Being a one-to-one school district for almost five years, with every student having an assigned device and their teachers being highly trained in a variety of technology platforms, they were able to quickly pivot to remote learning and continued to improve practices over time to better connect with students;
- The district collaborated with the YMCA and setup childcare for the essential workforce within their elementary school, serving approximately twenty to twenty-five children daily.

In addition to providing these three essential functions as a school district, according to Dr. Robbins, the caring faculty and staff became very creative, in order to maintain and build remote connections with their students, as they:

- Designed and delivered lawn signs to the house of each graduating senior of the Class of 2020
- Coordinated the students of their sophomore class sending positive message postcards to our graduating seniors
- Displayed senior portrait signs in front of the high school
- Continued to collect and virtually share student artwork
- Held a sixth grade "Chill & Chats" at the end of every week. These virtual meetings were offered for students to encourage relaxed social interaction and communication
- Created a collaborative playlist of music called "Quaren-tunes" to keep middle school students motivated and able to share their positivity with the Dutchmill community
- Held "Zoom Karaoke" with middle school chorus students as a fun way to bond and spend time together
- Honored their Lunch Heroes in food service, administrative professionals, teachers, and nurses
- Shared weekly videos such as Funny Friday, This Month's Birthdays, Virtual Spirit Week, and the Masked Reader in order to keep a sense of normalcy for their youngest students
- Honored spring athletes with daily features on social media
- Held an appreciation parade throughout the entire Dutchmill community, with the assistance of law enforcement
- Developed a special graduation event, all while staying within the parameters of promoting the health and safety of our school-community

According to Jack Robbins, as a school-community, they were faced with a global crisis; but they continually pivoted, were creative, and identified every single opportunity that they could, in order to be able to stay connected and remotely engaged with their students and families.

As Senator Kennedy dissected the Chinese word for crisis in 1959, *"In a crisis, be aware of the danger–but recognize the opportunity"*; timidly, Robbins' team embraced the challenges presented by the COVID-19 pandemic crisis, but made sure that they also enthusiastically recognized all of the new opportunities for them to embrace and connect with the families of their school-community. Dr. Robbins stated, "We will be stronger as we face the uncertain future together."

The superintendent continued, "Collectively, as we look to the future and reimagine what the landscape of schools will look like after this global health crisis, we turn to the lessons that we have already learned from the pivot to remote instruction." For quality input on what they need to consider for the future of learning, they turned to their teachers and once again utilized the survey tool of ThoughtExchange. The question posed to their teachers was,

"As you reflect on the past 10 weeks of Remote Teaching and Learning, please share specific thoughts of what areas need attention or further support, in order to provide for a smoother transition and/or continuance in the event that is what is expected of schools during the ongoing health crisis."

There were a total of 140 responses and over 261 thoughts generated by the participants. Themes focused around student and teacher expectations, professional development, technology, and health and safety. Some of the top thoughts were as follows:

I believe we need to better define student expectations in terms of engagement in distance learning. This is important for all stakeholders (student, parents/guardians, teachers, admin) so that all parties understand the base criteria for engagement

Parents need technology support by technology reps, not teachers. It is very very difficult for teachers to know all about the different apps and views of the parents' screens and be knowledgeable about technology.

Making sure that all students have the tech needed to be successful. If we move to distance learning- tech will be key to its success.

Professional development opportunities should be relevant/flexible to teacher needs and provide a choice to what they take. Teachers know their needs and should be able to decide what will work for them.

We need to focus on building relationships with students online next year, and training in best practices for doing this with new students. Many of us won't know our new students and learning does not thrive without relationships.

The home life of teachers needs to be considered. Teachers may be home with multiple children when a spouse is at work full time.

Social distant areas at Dutchmill needs to provide spaces for students to come in if needed. This assumes that they are "learning at home." Set up an area in the school where kids can be spaced apart, provided additional resources and teacher support.

As the leadership team at Dutchmill Central School District prepared to reopen for the fall of 2020, conversations were also taking place state-wide. In fact, on May 29, 2020, the New York State Education Department shared a PowerPoint (NYSED, 2020) with school districts, announcing a statewide taskforce and regional conversations about the reopening of schools.

The task force was comprised of parents, teachers, school and district leaders, school board members, and other interested parties. The belief was that by working together with these partners, we could ensure that the issues of health, safety, and educational equity would always come first. The guiding principles of the task force were:

1. The health, safety, and well-being of the children and adults in our schools is paramount.
2. We will always keep the issue of educational equity at the forefront of our thinking and decision-making.
3. We recognize that one size does not fit all. New York is a large state in population and size. We will always consider the tremendous diversity that exists among our people, our geographic regions, and our schools and school districts. While it is important to provide districts with guidelines and policies, it is important as well to give them appropriate leeway to develop creative solutions to their unique challenges.
4. We will enable and encourage districts to work directly with parents, teachers, administrators, and their local communities to develop and deliver workable solutions to their unique needs. We will succeed through our collective effort.
5. We will proceed with the understanding that planning for schools to reopen is not a one-time event. We will continuously monitor the situation and provide updated guidance, policies, and regulatory changes as the situation requires.

These conversations certainly guided how and when schools would reopen. This became the work of the Dutchmill Administrative Team, which was facilitated by Dr. Robbins, for the summer of 2020 and beyond.

REFLECTING ON THE COVID-19 CRISIS
AS SUPERINTENDENT OF SCHOOLS

The practice of reflection, in reaction to adverse events, allows school leaders to determine individually and collectively, the paths to move forward and become stronger together as a community and a society as a whole.

Although it is well documented that the practice of self-reflection is a positive activity for the successful development of leaders and "consequently, leadership development and good teaching practices depend on reflection-in-action" (Densten & Gray, 2001, p. 119), researchers have identified that, " . . . self-reflection is possibly a manager's least favorite activity" (Miller, 2012, p. 1). Researchers have concluded that leaders avoid reflection because " . . . leaders may be convinced by past successes of their invincibility and fail to consider other viewpoints, with possibly disastrous consequences" (Densten & Gray, 2001, p. 119).

There is a strong correlation however between those leaders that practice self-reflection and their levels of self-efficacy. In fact, a mixed methods study (Rabey, 2014) designed to effectively research potential correlations between the level of self-efficacy of school superintendents and their self-reflective practices provides valuable findings for school leaders.

The quantitative portion of the study utilized an online survey, which was completed by eighty-one superintendents from New York in the spring of 2013. The sample was a fairly accurate representation of the New York superintendents' population, and favorably compared to the superintendents' profile detailed in the 2012 New York State Council of School Superintendents SNAPSHOT publication (NYSCOSS, 2012).

One the quantitative component of the study was completed then a purposeful "Post-Hoc Focus Group" of eight superintendents reviewed the quantitative results. The researcher, employing a variety of qualitative techniques, concluded that the respondents supported the overall quantitative results and generally were not surprised by most of the findings. The overall study was designed around the following research question:

- Are self-reflective practices, superintendent profiles and school district demographics of New York State school superintendents a statistically significant predictor of their self-efficacy?

After evaluating the relationship between the self-efficacy of the New York superintendents of schools and their respective self-reflective practices, the findings were clear, as the combined independent variables (self-reflective practices) and predicted the outcome of the combined dependent variables (self-efficacy), that there was a statistically significant positive correlation between the New York school superintendents' self-reflective practices and their levels of self-efficacy.

Furthermore, the results showed that the higher the incidences of self-reflective activities by superintendents, the greater the tendency for them to have a higher level of self-efficacy within their practice which was consistent with previous similar studies (Miller, 2012; Schön, 1983).

Therefore, as the importance of a superintendent's self-reflective practices in relation to his or her success as a leader is better understood, coupled with this pandemic crisis as a backdrop, it was appropriate to review how superintendents coped through these uncertain times.

Subsequently, the author of this chapter decided to interview several of his colleagues who were practicing superintendents of schools who lead their school districts through the COVID-19 crisis. Those leaders were asked about their reflections on surviving as a leader during the COVID-19 crisis and reacting to the ever-fluid landscape.

Those superintendents performed their leadership roles in a crisis leadership environment that was influenced by the various executive orders of the governor, advice from the Department of Health, and the continuously adjusting regulations of the State Education Department, as well as the dismal fiscal budget outlook.

The thoughts of several of those interviewed superintendents are significantly summarized below by the following direct reflections of some of them:

There are a couple of things that really have jumped out at me as we have progressed through these unprecedented times:

6. Planning:The COVID-19 crisis presented us with an interesting paradigm shift as it relates to planning out solutions to the myriad of problems that were presented to us on a daily basis early on. Educators, by nature, are planners and administrators are long-range planners. The sheer volume of information and the rate at which we were having to process it forced us out of a proactive long-range planning mode into a reactive mode where we just solved one crisis at a time as they were presented to us.

7. Unified cooperation: One thing I found was that the magnitude of this crisis put things in perspective for our administrators, staff, and community, and by doing so many of the issues that were of paramount leading up to this crisis paled in comparison when stacked up against it. This allowed us to unify behind a common goal in a way we have never experienced. It was like capturing lightning in a bottle and it is something I have spoken on a number of times throughout in hopes of

fanning the flames behind this unified cooperation because the results, quite frankly, are awe-inspiring and worthy of replication once we are out of the crisis.

8. The importance of culture: I have been struck, a number of times, by the way similar messages and plans are received so differently from district to district. Part of this is due to communication style however, I believe the primary force behind it is the existence of a culture of trust. Where it exists, plans move forward without a hitch and entire school communities are content and are reaping the benefits.

The sampling of superintendents was then asked about their reflections on supporting the constituencies (students, parents, support staff, teachers, and administrators) within their school-community, in order to assist them in persevering through the COVID-19 health crisis. They were asked about approaches they used to personally cope with COVID-19 crisis. Several of them reflected that navigating through cancelled special events, losing contact time with other leaders for support, and an overall sense of helplessness were major stressors. However, the following statements illustrate those leaders' personal coping strategies:

Superintendent Smith, who is a superintendent of a small suburban school district, responded:

- BOE Meetings virtually/recorded and posted to website.
- Meal preparation available for pick-up and delivery. Assisting as you do in any way possible, preparing as well as delivering.
- Town Hall meetings via Zoom, just an open conversation answering folks questions and sharing the most up to date info.
- Virtual PTO meetings at the elementary level.
- Daily updates to website (COVID-19 tab), weekly messages from me to community.
- Teachers providing weekly welfare checks in addition to academic support.
- I/T support provided remotely.
- Ordering food for our family and staff from local business.
- Good well wishes and packages to first responders and local nursing homes.

Superintendent Brown, leading another small rural district, responded with:

Our messaging has been clear since day one . . . instruction and learning are important but can only exist when our students social, emotional, and mental health are tended to. We have set up multiple layers of support for our students, their families and our staff throughout the crisis in order to ensure that we accomplish this goal and it has been noticed and appreciated by all and we are now reaping the benefits on the backend.

In addition, Superintendent Smith pointed out several challenges:

- Perceived equity of all staff members being made whole throughout this time, as some are more available than others are.
- Food Service folks called in to work more than secretaries did. B&G department more than bus drivers etc.
- Unwillingness of employees (5–10%) to be available for students and parents "outside" of contractual day.
- Health and wellbeing of our own staff members, trying to keep spirits up. I attended department/grade level meetings on a regular basis (at least once a week).
- Navigating on site construction while following Exec. Orders.
- Preparing for 2020–21 (staffing, programs and budget). Preparing several plans with different funding scenarios.
- Graduation, prom, class trips (refunds or delay)

Finally, when the sampling of superintendents was asked how they are personally pushing through the crisis, how their normal schedule and work practices have been altered, adapted, or maybe even improved due to the crisis, and what they were doing for self-care, the answers were fairly consistent. Several of them cogently replied that they were:

- Exercising more and spending more time with their families
- Having more efficient meetings with their administrative teams and more focused communications with their colleagues around the region

In conclusion, it is clear that when leaders are reflective about their practices, especially during a crisis of this magnitude, they are more effective as a leader and able to be responsive to their school-communities as well as their own personal needs.

CHAPTER AUTHOR'S FINAL THOUGHTS

The prior historical review of district school leadership from March to September 2020 captures the very comprehensive and well-orchestrated efforts of school superintendents like Dr. Jack Robbins to promote caring teaching and learning during the initial stages of the COVID-19 global pandemic.

Dr. Robbins' focused approach and unbridled commitment to keeping the Dutchmill Central School District operating during the initial months of the COVID-19 crisis is definitely very laudable. This was the most unique and catastrophic time in educational history as schools were shuttered and the traditional teaching and learning structures of American schools were shuddered. This is a well-documented, classic journal type recording of the macro and micro events that impacted a school district and its people, things, and ideas and the acute leadership responses to them.

The procedures that were quickly established and employed by the superintendent and his team, in the face of uncertainty and non-helpful interference by other agencies, as well as the specific communication memos sent to school district employees, students, parents, and community members are excellent artifacts of their successful experience and will serve as models and templates for other leaders in the future.

School leadership is all about relationships and trust and it is obvious how building and maintaining those relationships and trusts in the Dutchmill Central School District was a priority for its leadership team. They confronted the initial impact of COVID-19 head on and survived and thrived as a caring educational institution that leaves an excellent history and replicable artifacts of its experiences.

George Santayana, Spanish-American philosopher, once admonished that "Those who cannot remember the past are condemned to repeat it." School leaders are encouraged to reflect about the forgoing history of a real school district and its very real superintendent, administrators, teachers, students, and parents who effectively weathered the turbulence of this global pandemic and shared their experiences so if similar perils occur in the future at least others will have a reference and pragmatic templates to help them survive their crisis.

However, as expected, school leaders utilized the guidance provided by the New York State Departments of Health and Education in August of 2020 and re-opened their schools under the set parameters identified. Schools welcomed students back in a variety of learning environments, from in-person instruction to hybrid platforms or fully remote options. Schools pivoted back and forth between these learning options throughout the school year depending on the local community's infection rates.

School leaders also needed to organize and perform on-site COVID-19 testing and, in some cases, even organized vaccination sites in the spring of 2021. School superintendents did whatever they could throughout the entire pandemic to provide for continuity of instruction and support of not only their students but the entire school community as they persistently and creatively conducted their leadership roles and responsibilities.

KEY PRAGMATIC LEADERSHIP
TAKEAWAYS FROM CHAPTER 2

- *Leaders need to be aware of potential outside influences that may have an impact on the educational organization.* They need to have a solid understanding of the leadership landscape, that factors in responses to such issues as health crises,' financial short falls, shifts in state and national educational platforms and political turmoil.
- *Leaders need to ensure that they are constantly responsive to their school-communities.* This is crucial when a crisis is unfolding. Leaders need to be aware of the needs of all constituencies, as they can be very different and in constant flux.
- *Leaders need to establish a high level of trust through consistent and effective communications.* Communications should be well-established prior to a crisis, but most prevalent during a crisis, as the school-community looks to knowing what is going on and what to expect from its leader. This consistent practice builds trust and reduces anxiety significantly.
- *Leaders need to involve a team of individuals when developing and implementing any contingency plans during a crisis.* This practice will ensure that plans are thoroughly reviewed by all constituencies and eventually supported when implemented.
- *Leaders need to appreciate that they do not have all of the answers.* This is especially true during a crisis and leaders need to be real and look for assistance wherever they can for the betterment of their school-community.
- *Leaders should never shy away from walking the walk.* When a crisis is unfolding, leaders need to be the first to respond and execute any task that is required to get through a crisis; from handing out meals, to training to administer COVID-19 tests, to covering classes when there is a substitute shortage, to picking up tests and distributing them to the school-community. Leaders should do first and then ask for assistance. This significantly increases the level of credibility in the view of all followers.
- *Leaders need to reflect about the significance to them personally and professionally of that Chinese statement that JFK employed, "In a crisis, be aware of the danger–but recognize the opportunity."* Leaders must be aware of the crisis that confronts them and their school district's people,

things, and ideas. However, they always need to stay attuned to the opportunities for further enhancement of the culture of their school community and the development of new and improved methods of teaching and learning that may truly be opportunities.

CHAPTER REFERENCES

DeCataldo, J. (2020). Correspondence from New York State Education Department on May 11, 2020, to all New York Superintendents of Schools.

Densten, I. L., & Gray, J. H. (2001). Leadership development and reflection: what is the connection? *International Journal of Educational Management*, 15(3), 119–124.

Kennedy J. (1959). https://www.relicsworld.com

Miller, P. (2012). Self-reflection: The key to effective leadership. Today's Manager. December 2011–January 2012.

New York State Council of School Superintendents (NYSCOSS). (2012). SNAPSHOT 2012 (8th ed.). Albany, NY.

New York State Education Department (NYSED) (2020). New York State Education Department's ReOpening Schools Task Force Recovering, Rebuilding & renewing the spirit of our schools. www.nysed.gov

NYSEDP12 (Personal Communication, March 30, 2020): Clarification on 180-day Requirements in Light of Executive Orders.

Rabey, J. R. (2014). The Relationship between the Self-Efficacy of New York State Superintendents of Schools And Their Self Reflective Practices Model.

Santayana, G. In *Wikipedia, The Free Encyclopedia*. Retrieved 20:28, February 10, 2022, from https://en.wikipedia.org/w/index.php?title=George_Santayana&oldid =1070837699

Schön, D. A., & DeSanctis, V. (1986). The reflective practitioner: How professionals think in action. *Journal of Continuing Higher Education*, 34(3), 29–30.

Tahoe, S., The New York State Education Department. (2020). Additional Guidance on Statewide School Closures Due to Novel Coronavirus (COVID-19) Outbreak in New York State.

Thoughtexchange. (n.d.). Retrieved April 30, 2020, from https://www.thoughtexchange .com/

Zucker, H. and Tahoe, S., New York State Department of Health and the New York State Education Department. (2020). School (PreK–12) Guidance: COVID-19.

Chapter 3

Constructing a Comprehensive Crisis Management Framework

Sunflower Unified School District Case Study

John E. McKenna and Walter S. Polka

This is a synthesized case study of the COVID-19 lived leadership experiences of several districtwide and building administrators who facilitated the survival and innovative expansion of teaching and learning in their respective school districts. This chapter contains practical information related to the actions and reactions of those school leaders who efficiently and effectively confronted the exigencies of the crisis during the 2020–2021 school year as reflected in this amalgamated case study.

The anonymous school district referenced in this case study, Sunflower Unified Central School District (SUCSD), is a prototypical large school district consisting of a student population of approximately ten thousand students housed in over a dozen pre-K–12 school buildings in a large metropolitan region of the Northeast United States. The school district is anonymous but the programs, procedures, and activities employed to confront the COVID-19 crisis are based on real-world administrative crisis management experiences collected from diverse contexts.

These experiences provide valuable reference templates that may be replicated by other educational leaders in similar crisis situations. The transformational leadership approaches, focused strategies, and pragmatic examples are "crisis-tested" models that promote adapting to and surviving unexpected and incredibly disruptive events in school district functions and operations.

The COVID-19 unprecedented global catastrophe resulted in multiple crises situations that most school leaders had never previously faced. As the pandemic of 2020 was identified and as it continued through to 2022, it created major new administrative problems for school leaders as they confronted multiple COVID-19 related crises at the local level and developed new options or made adaptations in their existing school operations and procedures to address them. Unfortunately, school leaders including those in the Sunflower Unified School District, were in unchartered territory and there was no playbook for them to follow to deal with such widescale crises.

Given the serious health and safety factors associated with the virus, many school districts were forced to close their doors and students had to learn from home. This made it imperative for districts to develop and adopt virtual learning models to deliver instruction to students.

Another factor that had a serious impact on schools was the concept of social distancing. Most states adopted the Centers for Disease Control and Prevention (CDC) Guidelines that specified that students needed to be always at least six feet apart in school. These guidelines further indicated that in certain areas and subjects such as lunchrooms and in gym classes the social distancing requirement had to be twelve feet.

Models for the Delivery of Teaching and Learning During the Crisis

These CDC guidelines posed great challenges for school leaders as it was necessary for them to work quickly to figure out how to teach and provide services to students. The guidance did not give many choices to the school districts. School district leaders basically had three models for teaching and learning to choose. Their options included: "Full Virtual Model," "Hybrid Model," or a "Hyflex Model."

A "Full Virtual Model" is when all students in the school learn virtually from home utilizing a laptop or chrome book type computer. The teacher provides a mix of synchronous and asynchronous instruction and students are expected to complete and submit all work online. In this model teachers can teach from home or at school depending on the school districts' rules and procedures.

In a "Hybrid Model," some students learn in person with their teachers on certain days, while other students work at home on asynchronous assignments. The students then flip roles on other days to allow those at home to come in for in person learning while others stay home and complete asynchronous work. This model was developed to allow students to attend school on some days and still be in alignment with the social distancing requirements.

A "Hyflex Concurrent Model" allows students at home and in person to learn together. Utilizing laptops, webcams, document cameras, smartboards and other technology, students at home and in person are able to experience the same instruction and lessons in real time.

This chapter analyzes the strategic and tactical decisions of the leaders of the Sunflower Unified School District in choosing appropriate instructional models for their students and the many challenges they confronted along the way. Since the district is a relatively large and diverse school district making changes required a significant amount of planning and coordination on the part of the central office administrators, school building principals, and their respective support staffs.

Preparing for School 2020

In the summer of 2020, school districts across New York State and the nation were preparing for the opening of school for the 2020–2021 school year. The New York State Education Department and Department of Health developed Guidance for schools regarding COVID-19 and mandated social distancing requirements for all schools. The guidance gave schools the option to develop in person, hybrid, hyflex, or fully virtual instructional models.

The authors of this chapter gathered information from several school districts and utilized their practical experience when writing this chapter. The school district of this case study developed a fully remote model and a hybrid model for elementary grades K–4. This allowed elementary parents to choose a model they felt worked best for their children.

However, they were not able to successfully choose and develop multiple instructional models for grades 5–12 by the beginning of school in September. As a result, all students at the Middle and High School levels had to receive instruction through a fully remote model.

The community was extremely upset that multiple models were not developed, and they demanded that the district provide some form of in-person instruction immediately. The Board of Education directed the superintendent to develop a plan that would solve this crisis and get students back in school as soon as possible.

TRANSITION PLANNING MATRIX: A STRATEGIC ACTION MODEL

The Sunflower Unified School District Superintendent immediately recognized that a strategic action model was necessary to attack the ongoing crisis. Accordingly, a multi-faceted strategic action model called "Transition

Planning Matrix" (figure 3.1), was developed. This plan consisted of multiple committees and empowered key individuals and stakeholders to assume leadership roles to actively engage them and facilitate their sense of ownership of the process.

The "Transition Planning Matrix" plan was designed to unify all stakeholders around a common vision, mission, goals and provides interactions to promote a strong moral purpose for the work that needs to be done in addressing student learning needs during an ongoing pandemic.

The plan was arranged as a flow chart with the "Leadership Team" at the top of the chart. The "Leadership Team" consisted of the Superintendent and the District-wide Assistant Superintendents. This group met daily to ensure all the details of the plan were properly developed and communicated to all stakeholders. They also made sure that all the committees and groups had the proper resources to complete their tasks.

The "Leadership Team" met on a regular basis with another key team created as part of the Transition Matrix. This team, the "Moving Forward Team," consisted of the principals, coordinators, and the assistant principals.

The "Moving Forward Team" was large, so portions of the team would meet separately as needed. However, the Leadership Team met daily with the building principals because they had an integral role in implementing the plan to confront specific context crisis in their school buildings. Sometimes these meetings were short "huddles," where they would touch base on what

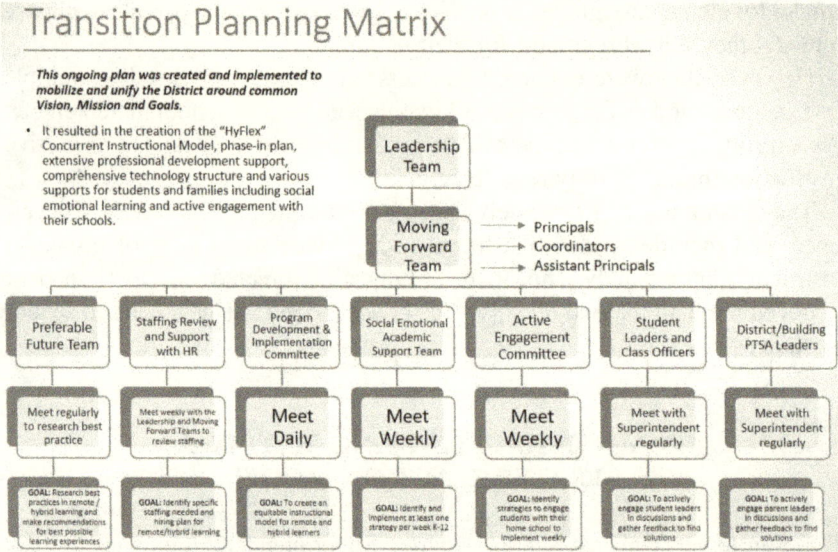

Figure 3.1   **Transition Planning Matrix**
McKenna and Polka, 2022

they were working on that day, but everyone felt that daily communication was essential in keeping all thirteen buildings in the district on the same page and moving forward.

The "Leadership Team" and members of the "Moving Forward Team" worked together to coordinate the four key committees and two key stakeholder groups that were embedded in the Transition Planning Matrix as illustrated in figure 3.1. Both teams also worked with the Human Resources Department to coordinate appropriate staffing to ensure the model could be implemented and run effectively.

Four Key Committees

The four key committees embedded in the "Transition Planning Matrix" designed to facilitate the school district's plan to abate the crisis and to maintain teaching and learning excellence were the: (1) Program Development and Implementation Committee, (2) Active Engagement Committee, (3) Social Emotional Academic Support (SEAS) Team, and the (4) Preferable Future Committee.

The Program Development and Implementation Committee was of crucial importance because this was the committee charged with developing an instructional model, and to assure that administrators, teachers, and support staff had the appropriate technology, infrastructure, and resources as well as the proper training and professional learning to successfully implement the emerging educational program for students.

This was a large committee and had over fifty members. It contained principals and key staff from each building, curriculum coordinators, technology integrators, staff developers, the assistant superintendents, and the superintendent.

This committee was under a great deal of pressure because the community and the Board of Education wanted a new instructional model as soon as possible. Other school districts in the region that had gone fully remote at the start of the 2020–21 school year, notified their communities that they would need at least five months to develop a program and would not be able to provide a different instructional model until January 2021.

The school superintendent of this case study school district told the members of the Program Development and Implementation Committee that waiting until January 2021 was unacceptable and re-emphasized that students and parents in this community needed this new instructional plan immediately and expected its implementation as soon as possible.

The superintendent emphasized the importance of this plan's start date by stating that, if necessary, the committee would meet every day until a final solution and an acceptable timeline, that would get students back in school by the end of October 2020, was developed and accepted by the school district's Board of Education.

The committee began work by researching numerous virtual learning models. They consulted with other school district personnel who were implementing virtual instructional models in the region and they collaborated with local university professors to learn about contemporary research regarding different virtual models implemented throughout the USA.

Upon completion of the comprehensive research review and intensive discussions, the committee established a list of "non-negotiables." These included the following: every student must have access to every course; students' schedules will not change; students will be taught by their regular teachers; and students, both at home and at school, will have the same high quality learning experiences as those at school.

Given these "non-negotiables" the committee made the choice to implement a "Hyflex Concurrent Model" where students at home and at school share the same learning experience at the same time only at different physical settings. This would allow all students to follow their regular class schedule and be able to experience learning activities in their respective courses.

This model also enables students at home to interact with those at school to help keep all students remain connected with their fellow students, teachers, and school environment. The committee brainstormed the components necessary to implement the model and called their plan the "Program Development and Implementation Plan."

To ensure the successful implementation of the plan, the committee members made sure that teachers and their support staff had the proper training and equipment to teach both in "face-to-face" classrooms and in the remote classrooms of students' homes. To accomplish this, some of the members worked on a professional learning plan to provide essential training to staff while others worked on securing the appropriate technology.

Some of the key components of the professional learning plan included that every staff member in grades 5–12 was required to take two mandatory courses as baseline training. Those courses were *Lesson Design* and *Community Building*. Also, every instructional staff member was offered training in how to utilize ZOOM and Google Classroom. Many staff were previously trained in Google Classroom and that was a big help as the district began implementation of the "Hyflex Concurrent Plan."

Another important element of the professional learning plan was the utilization of every Wednesday as designated time for professional learning. The students were given asynchronous work, and this allowed the entire staff in grades 5–12 to receive professional development and work together to plan instruction. Wednesdays became known as "Professional Learning Community Days."

The staff developers employed by the district created a catalogue of courses that teachers and their support staff could take to enhance their teaching approaches, differentiation of instruction techniques, and content knowledge.

The technology integrators were available to provide technical support and help individual teachers with their computer expertise. They were given time to coach and mentor other staff members who needed assistance in this new style of teaching and learning caused by the global pandemic. The entire staff felt that this time greatly enhanced the quality of work and helped people work together as effective instructional teams.

Those that worked on the technology side of the plan made sure that every student and teacher had a fully functional laptop or Chromebook with a working camera. The district had to order and prepare approximately five thousand new laptops in addition to preparing approximately six thousand existing laptops to ensure every student and teacher had an appropriate device. They also determined that every teacher should have an advanced digital camera that allowed them to record and post lessons on their websites.

This would allow students and parents to view and review instruction as needed. The committee further mandated that every classroom should have a mounted digital camera to provide a classroom view and a fully functional smartboard so the teacher and students in school could see and interact with those at home.

After the Program Development and Implementation Committee had determined the instructional model, professional learning plan, and technology plan, they needed to develop an implementation timeline. The superintendent had set the goal and expectation that this plan be fully implemented by the end of October 2020.

After many long days and countless hours of work the committee was able to fully implement all aspects of their approved Program Development and Implementation Plan by October 26, 2020. It was a total team effort and a monumental accomplishment.

The Active Engagement Committee was designed to find creative, meaningful, and fun ways to bring students, staff, and parents together and keep them actively engaged with their school during this unprecedented time of crisis. There were multiple instructional models at the elementary level, and they were different from the "Hyflex Concurrent Model" that was developed for grades 5–12.

At the elementary schools of this district, there were fully remote students who only received instruction online at home, as well as hybrid students who spent some days at school and other days at home. However, in grades 5–12 they spent the first two months of school as remote learners and then participated in the Hyflex Concurrent Model, where some students were in school and others were taught at home.

The superintendent believed that all students needed to feel connected to their school and classmates. The multiple models were disengaging students and families and making them feel disconnected from their schools. In addition, the superintendent firmly believed that all buildings in the district needed to be unified around a common moral purpose (Fullan, 2020).

The administrative leaders of the district, following the focus of the superintendent and the orientation of the Districts' Board of Education, were very concerned with their students' social and emotional well-being and wanted them to effectively connect with their school in positive ways. The intent was for students and their families to have fun, laugh, and feel good about their school as well as to know that they were appreciated and very much cared for in welcoming, human ways. This was the inspiration for the creation of the Active Engagement Committee.

The membership on this district-wide committee was purposely designed to be inclusive of all stakeholders in order to encourage and maximize participation. Staff, students, parents, and the assistant principals from all schools of the district were on the committee. The assistant principals played a key role on this committee and became the leaders for the building-based committees that would spin off of the district committee.

The original committee met and decided that there should be both district-wide activities and individual building-based activities. To accomplish this, each building was directed to form a building-based "Active Engagement Committee." These building-based committees were led by the assistant principals. Each building-based committee was also inclusive to all stakeholders and included staff, students, and parents.

The charge for the building-based committees was straightforward. They were to develop activities that creatively engaged their students and families on a weekly basis. They were charged by the superintendent to create and implement plans at each building and then report their progress back monthly to the district committee.

This became a very positive process where the members of building committees shared ideas, best practices, and, oftentimes, cooperatively planned to properly implement similar activities. These activities connected students and their families to their schools in fun and meaningful ways. The weekly, building-based activities were well-received and, truly, very much appreciated by all stakeholders.

The focused goal for the district-wide committee was to bring together all district school buildings and unite the entire district with a common vision and moral purpose. To accomplish this, they developed a multi-faceted strategy. First, they wanted to create a slogan, catch phrase, or hashtag that would serve as a unifying message for the community. Students from all district schools submitted ideas. Students and staff from across the district voted on the unifying message.

Once the message was determined, another district contest was held to turn the slogan into a visual piece of art that could be put on shirts, posters, stickers, and magnets and displayed across the district and community. Each school had their own contest and then they submitted their winners to the district committee for a district-wide vote.

Nearly all ten thousand students participated in the final vote and a district-wide symbol of unity was adopted. It was put on shirts, hoodies, hats, and bumper stickers and displayed across the district and at school district events. It was a very effective unifying message that was embraced by the entire community.

Next, the district-wide committee created a community service project to unite all school buildings around the concepts of empathy and caring for children in our community. The superintendent and the committee members discussed the importance of reaching out to others less fortunate in times of crisis. They considered multiple possibilities for this project, and after discussions decided to partner with a well-known charity for school children with serious illnesses.

This community service project was embraced by the school leaders because the district had several students with serious illnesses and the committee wanted to help students within their own community. The committee's goal was to unite and ensure that all students were supported. This project also aligned perfectly with the moral purpose of unifying the district and caring for others in the community (Fullan, 2020).

Crucial to the success of this project was the mobilization and involvement of student leaders at the high school level. The district has multiple high schools and the student leaders at all of them expressed their interest to participate in this project with the superintendent.

In addition, the superintendent was working with two groups of students from the various high schools. One group was known as the "Superintendent High School Advisory Team," and another group consisted of the class officers from the senior, junior, sophomore, and freshman classes. The superintendent decided to combine them and form the "District Student Leadership Team." This group had over one hundred students who were highly motivated to get involved (see figure 3.2).

Students were given the opportunity to participate in the Active Engagement Committee and other committees as well. They were instrumental in the success of the community service project. As part of this project, they developed weekly themes around the positive character traits of empathy, caring, giving, compassion, helpfulness, proactivity, good citizenship, and being respectful and responsible.

Student Leadership Structure

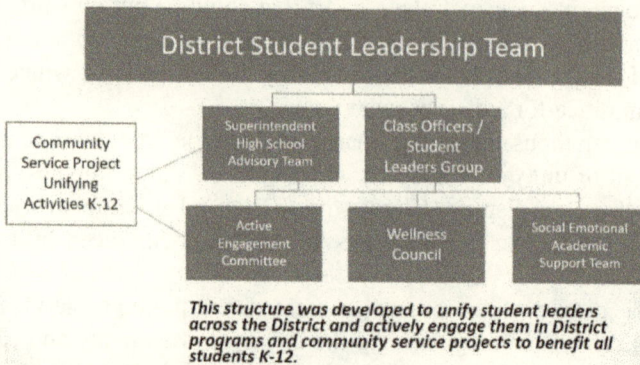

This structure was developed to unify student leaders across the District and actively engage them in District programs and community service projects to benefit all students K-12.

Figure 3.2   **Student Leadership Structure**
McKenna and Polka, 2022

The students then created videos that illustrated those traits in action. They came up with the idea of showing different videos in all district schools on a weekly basis. These videos were very motivational to the students and staff at each school and communicated a powerful message of caring and unity.

Additionally, with the help of the student leaders, the community service project was enormously successful and raised over $100,000. Because of the efforts of the Active Engagement Committee, students identified with serious illnesses were supported, their needs were met, and the entire district was united under a common moral purpose.

The Social Emotional Academic Support Team (SEAS)

The Social Emotional Academic Support Team was formed to provide social, emotional, and academic support for students who may have been individually struggling during the pandemic. The committee members also provided and facilitated counseling, assistance, and professional development for staff as necessary. The COVID-19 pandemic revealed the importance of providing additional support for students and staff, and this committee delivered a full court press of initiatives.

The district-wide SEAS Team was composed of district-level coordinators, building-level administrators, key support staff, and students on the District Student Leadership Team that represented all high schools in the district. Members of this committee began meeting weekly in the beginning of the 2020–2021 school year because of the crisis, but eventually transitioned to monthly meetings as the year progressed.

The SEAS Team established some key strategies that became standard practices throughout the district. One of these practices was conducting *daily wellness checks*. These checks were conducted by teachers to see how the students were feeling and to see if they could provide any support or assistance (Noddings, 1992). These checks helped to identify multiple students who identified that they needed additional social, emotional, or academic support.

Another practice initiated by the SEAS Team members was the regular and frequent use of *community circles.* Using this technique, teachers were able to engage in whole class or small group activities to discuss the following with students: "How are you feeling?"; "What's on your mind?"; "What's is going well?"; "Where are you struggling?"; "How can you support each other to survive and thrive during this unexpected crisis?"

This technique gave the teachers a great deal of flexibility to adjust the topics discussed in the circles based on the needs of the students. Many teachers utilized this practice daily and every teacher was expected by their administrators to implement the practice at least weekly. Individual students were trained to run these circles at the high school, and this turned out to be a very effective empowering strategy that actively engaged students and helped them trust the process.

The SEAS Team was also instrumental in planning and organizing key *professional learning opportunities* for the staff. This training was important to allow the staff to address the non-traditional instructional issues they were encountering.

Some key programs and trainings that were made available for the staff included: restorative practices, mindfulness, trauma and trauma informed care, and the Collaborative Academic Social Emotional Learning (CASEL) program. The CASEL program provided teachers with practical examples of how they may embed social emotional learning in all lessons across the curriculum (CASEL.org, 2022).

The SEAS Team was also in constant contact with the wellness teams at each building. Each building had representation on the SEAS Team from their building-based wellness team. This ensured that the district initiatives were being heard and implemented in each building. This was especially important for the implementation of coordinated professional learning activities on Wednesdays.

As previously mentioned, Wednesday afternoons were utilized by the district for professional learning. Coordination between the district and buildings was crucial to ensure that necessary, appropriate, and consistent training was implemented. The SEAS team was integral to the success of this process.

The Preferable Future Committee was responsible for envisioning the next steps in the process. This committee was charged with researching and investigating best practices in remote, hybrid, and hyflex learning and to make recommendations for the future. It was unknown at the time when students could return to full in-person learning, and this committee was exploring the possibilities for creating a preferable future to make this happen.

The committee's work was cut short when it was decided by state and local authorities that students could return to in person instruction. Many members of the committee felt that the work should have been allowed to continue. They believed that cultivating new ways of teaching and learning needed to be explored to ensure students received the highest quality learning experiences and were prepared for the future that may be significantly altered because of crises like the global pandemic.

Two Key Stakeholder Groups

The two key stakeholder groups that were essential to the successful development and implementation of the Transition Matrix Plan were student and parent leaders. Their input and participation were crucial throughout the process.

The Student Leaders at all of the district's high schools played a crucial role in the formulation of the original plan. At the onset of the crisis, the superintendent met with them weekly to hear their concerns and ideas for moving forward.

A key component that evolved from their input was that students definitely wanted to have access to all courses, be taught by their regular teachers, and be able to interact with all of their classmates. This perspective was crucial to the establishment of the Hyflex Concurrent Model and the elements included in the Program Development and Implementation Plan.

The weekly meetings with the students lasted until the plan was implemented, and the students had multiple committees in which they could participate and continue to provide input to their school district.

The students also expressed the desire to be actively engaged in helping their fellow students and the district come together during a difficult time. Their voices and passion to help were the inspiration for the district wide community service project and the creation of the District Student Leadership Team (figure 3.2).

The District Student Leadership Team provided the students with multiple committees and activities in which they could participate at the district and building levels. These committees included the building and district-based "Active Engagement Committee"; the "Social Emotional Academic Support Team"; and the "District Wellness Council"; and the "Wellness Team" in each school.

An amazing number of students participated in these initiatives and their ideas were the driving force behind so many successful activities that helped students and their parents and teachers cope throughout this protracted pandemic. The active participation and leadership from students made an incredible and undeniable difference in the successful implementation of the Transition Planning Matrix strategic plan and definitely had a major positive impact on the culture of the district during this ongoing global health crisis.

Parent Leaders also played a key role in providing crucial information that was essential to the successful development and implementation of the strategic plan. The involvement and active engagement of parents is crucial for the successful roll-out of any educational visionary plan (Blankenstein, 2013). At the beginning of the crisis when all the students in grades 5–12 had to learn remotely, the superintendent immediately began meeting with the leaders from the schools' Parent Teacher Student Associations (PTSA) on a weekly basis.

Input from parents and PTSA members provided valuable information as well as direction to district leaders. These sessions were engaging opportunities for parents to express their concerns, thoughts, feelings, and opinions about school operations during this crisis. The superintendent and other district-wide administrators met with the PTSA leaders weekly until the plan was successfully implemented and then continued to meet on a monthly basis after that.

The PTSA district leaders were also liaisons for the other parents in each school building. They surveyed their membership across the district and presented the superintendent with a document that contained the concerns and suggestions from all buildings. This document was very important because it provided feedback and clearly showed the major concerns of parents.

The District Leadership Team and Moving Forward Team both used this information to develop a Frequently Asked Questions (FAQ) document that was made available on the school district's website. An analysis of the FAQs and answers made it perfectly clear to school district leaders that the parents were aligned with the students and that they wanted to see similar learning specifics in a plan moving forward.

The parents made it very clear that they wanted their children to have access to all courses and they wanted them to have their regular teachers. They also wanted them to be able to interact with their classmates as much as possible. The parents further stressed the importance of developing and implementing a plan as quickly as possible. Their input was indispensable in the development of the Program Development and Implementation Plan.

The parent input was also fundamental to the implementation of the plan. Based on their recommendations when the plan was being implemented, each school held three virtual forums where parents could ask questions and receive necessary information on the details of the plan and how it would affect their children.

Their input also helped the principals of each school create informational videos and screencasts that provided specific information on the plan. These informational videos were posted on each school's website as a resource for parents. Many parents expressed their appreciation for these resources and for the ability to have input in the process.

The Important Role of Principals, Assistant Principals, and Coordinators

The leadership and active participation of the principals, assistant principals, and coordinators were essential to the successful development and implementation of the plan. They led committees at the district and building levels and willingly shared their skills, talents, and expertise.

They were an integral part of every discussion, and their feedback was essential in the formation of every decision related to school district operations during the continuing pandemic crisis. They were an indispensable part of the team and were genuinely empowered to participate in the shared decision-making process to find creative solutions to solve the crisis.

Many of these administrators commented that being empowered and having input gave them a sense of ownership and motivated them to want to go the extra mile and help as much as they could. They appreciated that their opinions and ideas were respected, and they felt a professional responsibility and a sense of honor to help the cause.

Multiple administrators also expressed that they had a strong belief in the moral purpose of the work and believed that their contributions would have a direct positive effect on the lives of their students.

The plan they helped create was one that they intensely believed in and felt very much connected to the implementation of all its components. They expressed how important it was that all district stakeholders were united as a team around the same vision, mission, and goals and were given the professional respect to contribute and lead during the crisis.

THE IMPORTANCE OF A STRONG CRISIS COMMUNICATION PLAN

Every school district should have an established communication plan; however, it is imperative to have a comprehensive communication strategy during a crisis. A communication plan is essential to establish strong relationships and trust with all stakeholders (Covey, 2006). The following are specific, successful methods that were implemented by various school districts studied, but especially the case study district of this chapter.

Daily Video Updates—At the onset of the crisis, it is crucial to get information out to all stakeholders as soon as possible and daily. The entire community wants and needs to know what is going on, is there a plan, and how the plan will address the situation. Transparency is essential to build trust and support for the plan and to calm the fears and anxiety that come with a crisis.

The authors of this chapter, as well as other educational leaders who successfully led schools and school districts during this crisis, emphasize that researchers have identified that effective leaders utilize daily video messages. Those videos highlighted key information and shared this information consistently through various modes of communication including the district website, Twitter, Facebook, text messages, and email.

Daily video updates should be utilized until the initial impact of the crisis subsides or a plan to address the exigencies of the situation is fully implemented. This period of time may last weeks or months, depending on the crisis. For example, former New York State Governor Andrew Cuomo did 111 consecutive daily briefings for the COVID-19 pandemic. Once school leaders determined that a daily message is no longer necessary, the messages should be transitioned to a weekly video message.

The Weekly Video Message—This message needs to be more focused on the implementation of the plan and the desired future outcomes and goals. This video message should show the plan in action and be on location in various school buildings as much as possible.

The message should feature real people implementing the plan and talking about how they are bringing the plan to life. These real-life images in the case study district, provided powerful messages that the ideas talked about in the daily messages were workable, real, and true solutions people could believe in.

Hold Weekly Informational Sessions with Opportunity for Q&A—A proactive leader must make the time to hold informational sessions with key stakeholder groups. The participants should be part of a legitimately recognized stakeholder group with duly elected members (i.e., the PTSA, student government). Members of these groups should be selected because they represent their constitutes.

These meetings should be in person if feasible but can be held virtually if necessary. At these meetings, the leader should share as much information as possible about the situation and the plan to address the crisis. The leader should also allow the stakeholders the opportunity to ask questions or present questions from the people they represent.

The leader should answer the questions as honestly and transparently as possible and make sure that all questions are turned into an FAQ that can be posted on a website for the entire community to access. These weekly meetings should continue until the crisis plan has been fully implemented. Then the meetings should move to monthly meetings.

Monthly Informational Sessions with Key Stakeholders—After the initial shock of the crisis subsides and the plan to address the matters at hand are being implemented, a leader can transition the weekly meetings into monthly information sessions. These sessions can be held either in person or virtually and are designed to give progress reports to the community. As the crisis subsides, these meetings will eventually be phased out at the discretion of the leader.

Hold Informational Forums at Specific Sites by the Building Administrators—In school districts it is imperative to hold informational sessions at each school conducted by the principal and members of the staff. Parents want to know how the plan to address the crisis will impact their child and individual school.

Principals are the educational leaders who best know the people, things, and things of their respective school buildings and effective principals are usually trusted by their parents. They are credible messengers to deliver information and answer specific questions about how the plan will affect all aspects of their child's school, for example bussing, lunches, special areas, homework, and extracurriculars. Global leadership researchers Kouzes and Posner (2017), reinforce the significance of such credible messengers when they contend that, if individuals don't trust the messenger, then they won't trust the message.

Create Site Specific Informational Presentations—Each school or site should create presentations such as informational videos, screencasts, and/or PowerPoints showing and explaining the unique changes caused by the crisis and being implemented at building levels. These presentations are most powerful when they chronicle the exact steps and procedures students, and staff must follow throughout a typical day.

They should highlight every aspect of the "new" education approaches being implemented as well as the challenges students and staff will face throughout each instructional day. Seeing the actual site and how things will be implemented helps to calm the fears of students, parents, and staff, helps relieve anxiety, and answers most questions people have.

These presentations should be proactively sent to families and staff and posted on each school's website as well as the district website before every aspect of the plan is implemented.

Update the District Website and All Building Websites—This is an essential step in an effective communication plan. Most people will initially look for important information on the website. The home page should clearly highlight the most important information and be simple to navigate. New pages will need be created to highlight specific actions of the plan, and links to pertinent presentations and data.

The district and individual building websites should direct all stakeholders to the same, updated information. Each site needs to link to a common page that houses the updates and information. IT teams need to work in conjunction with the Communication department to ensure all websites are updated continuously and simultaneously.

Develop Weekly District and Building Newsletters—To ensure effective and consistent communication across a district, the authors of this chapter, as well as others, recommend the development of weekly digital newsletters from each school building and the district office.

These newsletters should contain the most important and pertinent building-specific information. Some additional items to include are a weekly message from the principal, curriculum and program highlights, student spotlight(s), extracurricular activities, school concerts and events, and current information from the district.

CHAPTER AUTHORS' FINAL THOUGHTS

This chapter presented and analyzed specific initiatives and strategies that educational leaders have implemented as they confronted the ongoing COVID-19 pandemic crisis in real school districts. The chapter authors analyzed the specifics of a strategically constructed framework that other current or aspiring leaders may wish to utilize and adapt to meet the needs, problems, and issues that arise from all unexpected crisis situations.

It is crucial that leaders address the crisis head on with a strategic action plan such as the "Transition Planning Matrix" plan depicted in figure 3.1 of this chapter. This plan must contain clear vision, mission, and goals and be built upon the foundation of a strong moral purpose. The staff must believe in the plan and understand its importance, or they will not be willing to actively engage in the work to bring it to fruition.

The leader needs to create teams and committees to address the goals of the strategic action plan and people must be mobilized to participate and lead the work that must be done. The leader must match the skills and talents of the staff to the tasks that need to be completed. Getting people on the "right seats on the bus" is crucial to the success of the plan (Collins, 2001).

These teams are also essential to actively engage people and help them to take ownership of the problems and solutions that must be solved and generated during a crisis. It is also crucial that the leader becomes directly involved in all aspects of the plan and works with all the committees, teams, and staff to help complete the tasks. Working directly with the district stakeholders and sharing responsibility for the success of the plan is a key in fostering positive relationships and building trust.

Finally, it is imperative that the leader construct a comprehensive communication plan. This plan must address immediate issues and long-term goals. It should contain daily and weekly updates and provide clear, timely, accurate information. The plan should also address meetings with key stakeholder groups and provide opportunities for informational forums so the community can ask questions and provide feedback and suggestions for improvement.

The communication plan should implement a full court press approach and utilize all forms of social media as well as traditional methods to communicate to the public. Some of the key methods highlighted in this chapter are the use of daily and weekly videos, Twitter, Facebook, Instagram, multiple community forums, school and district websites, and the creation of weekly digital newsletters from each school and the district office.

Communication cannot be taken for granted. It must be intentionally and strategically planned. It is essential to disseminating important information and is the foundation for building relationships and trust with the community.

KEY PRAGMATIC LEADERSHIP TAKEAWAYS FROM CHAPTER 3

- *Leaders need to develop a clear strategic action plan to address the crisis:* They recognize the importance of having a strong plan with a clear vision, mission, and goals. This is imperative to give guidance to the staff but also instills confidence and hope in the successful outcome of the plan—internally and externally, and with all stakeholders.
- *Leaders need to establish and communicate the moral purpose of the plan:* They understand that people will not follow a plan in which they do not they believe. The leader must establish the importance of the mission, explain why it is essential and how it will impact the lives of the students, parents, staff, and community.
- *Leaders must create committees and teams that align with the plan:* They realize that specific groups need to be formed that directly align with the work that needs to be completed. This is a key structural component of the strategic action plan. The precise teams with the appropriate focus must be formed to complete the right work (Marzano, 2005).
- *Leaders must mobilize and empower people:* They recognize that they cannot do it alone and that people must be actively engaged in the development and implementation of the plan. It is crucial that they know the individual skills, talents, and expertise of the staff to match them with

the appropriate team. It is also essential in selecting and empowering the right people to take on leadership roles.

- *Leaders must be directly involved and have constant communication with the teams:* They know that their direct involvement and visibility communicates a powerful message to the staff. Working with the staff builds relationships and forms bonds of trust. Working directly on teams and committees guarantees timely and accurate communication and allows for proactive decisions to be made.
- *Leaders must develop a comprehensive communication plan:* They realize that accurate, timely, transparent communication is a must during a crisis. They set up a system that provides daily, weekly, and monthly communication using all modes of social media, online and through traditional methods of communication. They further realize that communication must come from all levels of the organization and set up systems that allow for district and building level communication.

REFERENCES

CASEL (2022). *Collaborative Academic Social Emotional Learning.* CASEL.org.

Collins, J. (2001). *Good to great: Why some companies make the leap and others don't.* New York: HarperCollins Publishers.

Covey, S. M. R. (2006). *The speed of trust: The one thing that changes everything.* New York, NY: Free Press.

Blankstein, A. (2013). *Failure is not an option: Six principles that advance student achievement in highly effective schools.* Thousand Oaks, California: Corwin and The HOPE Foundation.

Fullan, M. (2020). *Leading in a culture of change.* Hoboken, NJ: Jossey-Bass.

Kouzes, J. & Posner, B. (2017). *The leadership challenge: How to make extraordinary things happen in organizations.* Hoboken, N.J: Wiley & Sons Publishers.

Marzano, R., Waters, T. & McNulty, B. (2005). *School leadership that works: From research to results.* Alexandra, VA: Association for Supervision and Curriculum Development.

Noddings, Nel (1992). *The challenge to care in schools: an alternative approach to education,* New York: Teachers College.

Chapter 4

Instructional Leadership

The Critical Spark to Lead Meaningful Educational Change

Monica J. VanHusen and Walter S. Polka

"It is not the strongest of the species that survives, nor the most intelligent. . . . It is the one that is the most adaptable to change."*

SPARKING INSTRUCTIONAL CHANGES DURING CRISES AND SUSTAINING THEM AFTERWARD

Instructional leaders spark educational innovations throughout their career for deeper learning and to effectively manage appropriate curriculum experiences for students. As former first lady Rosyln Carter once stated, "A leader takes people where they want to go. A great leader takes people where they don't necessarily want to go, but ought to be" (Graciousquotes.com). Great instructional leaders also recognize that people, things, and ideas related to

---

*This quote, often attributed to Charles Darwin (*On the Origin of the Species*, 1859), is not a direct quote from his seminal work. Leon C. Megginson, Professor of Management and Marketing at Louisiana State University, paraphrased Darwin's theoretical concepts and attributed that now famous statement to Darwin on page 4 in a 1963 article in *Southwestern Social Science Quarterly*, 44(1): 3–13. Subsequently, the above statement has been listed as a Darwin quote in several venues and publications including: at the Field Museum of Natural History in Chicago and emblazoned on the floor of the California Academy of Sciences in San Francisco. However, it is a valid paraphrase of Darwin's key evolution concept for biological and cultural change comprehension.

education need to adapt to changes, a la Charles Darwin (1859), in order to effectively survive and thrive.

This is a pragmatic definition of a truly effective instructional leader who intentionally builds teacher efficacy and agency to create and facilitate responsive and reliable curricular and instructional practices that help students be prepared for their future by igniting passions for learning excellence in any contextual setting, including crisis situations.

Educators who are true instructional leaders in their respective organizations may be recognized by a myriad of other designated roles and responsibilities that they officially possess such as: the superintendent of schools; deputy superintendent of curriculum and instruction, assistant superintendent for human resources, director of special education, instructional technology coaches, coordinator of specific content areas, professional staff developers, building principals, assistant principals, department chairs, teacher team leaders, and classroom teachers.

However, no matter their official organizational title and responsibilities, educators who are identified as "true instructional leaders" are those whose heart and soul are passionately and perpetually involved in career-long teaching and life-long learning experiences such as personified by Mr. Chips in the classic 1939 film, *Goodbye, Mr. Chips.*

Contemporary avid instructional leaders, who have that "Chips" in their heart, are the superintendent of schools or other central office administrators who engage with students in a variety of learning settings, often teaching classes to satisfy their quest to be "in the learning environment" or building principals, assistant principals, department chairs who relish the opportunities to more than "visit classrooms" but actually intensely interact with students as their "teacher for the day."

All educators have the potential to become such fervently motivated and purposefully devoted instructional leaders but those who truly possess the love for teaching and learning ubiquitously express it daily in their decisions and actions, and thus become the "sparks" for meaningful changes in teaching and leaders, especially during crisis situations.

However, effective instructional leaders need to possess a mindset that focuses their passion on three key dimensions of instructional leadership to appropriately lead this change and promote adaptions to teaching and learning based on the realities of their respective contexts. These three traditional dimensions are: (1) defining the school's mission, (2) managing the instructional program(s), and (3) promoting a positive school learning climate (Hallinger, 2005).

Operating within these three dimensions, instructional leaders can spark educators they supervise or coordinate to move toward collaborating, creating, and maintaining responsive and reliable curriculum for students at any time, but most especially during crisis situations. Instructional leadership focusing on these three dimensions helps teachers adapt to current exigencies and takes them where they ought to be with curriculum and instruction plans designed to create deeper and more meaningful learning experiences for their students.

Instructional leadership rapidly became a prominent focus within schools and school districts as educators navigated through the turbulence caused by the 2020–21 COVID-19 punctuated equilibrium. It should be noted that a punctuated equilibrium is defined as: an evolutionary trend that is characterized by long periods of stability in the characteristics of an organism, including social institutions such as schools, and short periods of rapid change during which new forms appear (Merriam-Webster, 2020).

Contemporary instructional leaders needed to constantly reflect upon and effectively utilize their respective organizational knowledge, professional skills, and personal dispositions related to promoting and implementing curriculum designs and instructional plans in a metaphorical manner similar to that proclaimed by Mark Twain as he assessed the pervasive piloting skills of Mississippi River boat captains in 1886:

> *Two things seemed pretty apparent to me. One was, that in order to be a Mississippi River pilot a man had got to learn more than any one man ought to be allowed to know; and the other was, that he must learn it all over again in a different way every 24 hours* (Twain, p. 35).

Accordingly, two things seemed pretty obvious for instructional leaders practicing in both the 2020–21 and the 2021–22 school years: They needed to know more than any one person ought to know about the people, things, and ideas of their respective schools and school systems to "spark the changes" necessary to address the educational turbulence caused by the crisis at their doorsteps. And they needed to learn it again every twenty-four hours since navigating in this type of unexpected turbulence of global change required a focus on continuously learning and being adaptable with a positive professional mindset so that their schooling processes could survive.

New Blended Learning Opportunities

The COVID-19 pandemic made it necessary for blended learning opportunities to be implemented in fall 2020 in most schools in the United States. As defined by Krueger from the International Society of Technology Educators (ISTE) blog (2014), "blended learning" is any time a student learns at least, in part, at a supervised brick-and-mortar location away from home and at least, in part, through online delivery with some element of student control over time, place, path, and pace.

There was an acute need for a coherent instructional system during this significantly new blended learning hybrid experience in K–12 public education promulgated by the impact of the global pandemic. This was a major change in the traditional.

During this crisis experience, instructional leaders needed to comprehensively employ and intensively monitor, as well as continuously adapt, their applications of the three dimensions of effective instructional leadership based on evolving contextual realities to inspire teachers to create agency for this new type of blended learning format. Accordingly instructional leaders, whose schools and school systems were successful during this crisis, worked comprehensively and intensely in:

- Defining the school's "new" mission
- Managing the "emerging" instructional program(s)
- Promoting a positive "blended" school learning climate

Subsequently, when employing the above three dimensions during this crisis, highly effective instructional leaders consistently demonstrated courage, accepted challenges, and inspired others as articulated in various school leadership references (Fullan & Kirtman, 2019, p. 48). Instructional leadership has always been an important part of education, but now with the need to create new blended learning experiences for students as well as to maintain instructional fidelity to program expectations, it required intensive courage and continuous adaptations, as instructional leaders were required to navigate their schools in this "new normal" of public education.

Even though educators entered a new state for public education with blended learning opportunities, it was still necessary for them to assure their school public and their respective state agencies that the prescribed curriculum is guaranteed and viable for all students. They needed to affirm that their district's fidelity to the opportunity to learn for all students, as specifically guaranteed by state and federal guidelines, was pre-eminent whether the curriculum and instruction were delivered online, face to face, or in a blended combination of the two (Marzano, 2003).

Educational Equity in a Crisis Setting

This guarantee was further reinforced by statewide instructional leaders as reflected by the document produced, titled *The Aspen Education & Society Program and the Council of Chief State School Officers* in 2017, wherein it was stated that "educational equity means that every student has access to the educational resources and rigor they need at the right moment in their education across race, gender, ethnicity, language, disability, sexual orientation, family background and/ or family income" (p. 5).

However, a key step toward educational equity for any local instructional leader to make, especially in a crisis situation, was to ensure that appropriate and challenging curricula and instructional practices are guaranteed for all students no matter which school within the district a student attends or which mode of curriculum and instructional delivery is chosen for them.

Another important step is for local instructional leaders is to assure, through comprehensive supervision and appropriate assessment, that teachers are not dismissing material because of lack of knowledge, perceived intrinsic importance, or lack of time. This became even more important as the movement towards blended learning experiences was further demanded by the social, economic, and educational turbulence caused by the initial phases of the 2020 pandemic.

Instructional leaders needed to provide clear guidance to teachers regarding the content to be addressed in specific courses and at specific times (Marzano, 2003, p. 24). This guidance must be part of a coherent system for blended learning: curriculum, instruction, and assessments, that promote consistency in learning objectives as well as deep and meaningful learning experiences for all students.

Also, Marzano confirms that there are additional action steps that can be taken to guarantee that the curriculum is equitable for all no matter the time, place, or contextual situations. These actions steps are:

- Identifying and communicating the content that is considered essential
- Ensuring that the essential content can be addressed in the amount of time available via sequencing and organizing the essential content so students have ample opportunity to learn
- Ensuring that teachers address essential content
- Protecting instructional time that is needed (Marzano, 2003, p. 24)

Instructional leaders throughout the country employed the above action steps during the pandemic crisis, to confidently assure their respective stakeholders with that meaningful curriculum and effective instruction are appropriately guaranteed whether delivered in face-to-face, blended, or completely in online formats. Traditional instruction in schools needed to be significantly altered as dictated by the exigencies caused by the COVID-19 pandemic. And, the previously well-established approaches to teaching and learning needed to be adapted in order for the system of education to survive.

COHERENCE BETWEEN CURRICULUM,
INSTRUCTION, AND ASSESSMENTS

An instructional leader needs to create coherence between curriculum, instruction, and assessment to ensure student opportunity for success no matter the context nor the educational delivery system. Coherence is the shared depth of understanding about the purpose and nature of the work in the minds and actions of individuals and teams engaged in teaching and learning (Fullan & Kirtman, 2019).

Coherence is not a structured strategy delivered and owned by the instructional leader. To undertake a coherent system an instructional leader needs to work within a coherent framework which focuses on four key components. These four components, according to contemporary researchers, are:

- Focused directions
- Cultivating collaborative cultures
- Securing accountability
- Deepening learning (Fullan & Kirtman, 2019)

As instructional leaders worked toward coherence within more blended and virtual learning settings because of required school closures, they needed to cooperatively work with all stakeholders of their respective school district including: students, teachers, administrators, parents, and community members to adapt the mission and vision of their schools based on the realities of the crisis situation.

Each of the four components are correlated with the other three and must be addressed simultaneously and continually, while the instructional leader both activates and connects the four components (Fullan & Kirtman, 2019). Obviously, this correlation required cognitive knowledge and emotional dispositions, similar to those reflected in the Mark Twain analysis of the Mississippi River boat captain, as they continuously learned to adapt curriculum and learning practices during this crisis.

Undertaking instructional leadership within these four components starts with focusing professional direction on the school and/or district's mission. To focus direction, "an instructional leader has to have the courage to 'push' and 'pull' the status quo to effectively challenge, but also gain feedback, while also gaining an understanding and creating focus for the stakeholders" (Fullan & Kirtman, 2019, p. 18). After challenging and gaining feedback, the instructional leader needs to simplify the focus.

For leaders of a school system to maintain focus on the highest priorities, they must simplify and repeatedly clarify them so everyone in the organization knows implicitly what to do and what not to do (Schmoker, 2018). As more school organizations moved into more of a blended learning format for instruction and assessment throughout the United States, it was vital for instructional leaders to have the courage to continue to challenge the status quo and focus instruction efforts on innovations and continuous adaptations for student success.

Simplifying a mission often started, during the initial stages of this crisis situation, with a review and analysis of the school improvement plan process in most local school districts. Instructional leaders needed to be goal oriented and focused on improving student academic success by aligning strategies and activities to re-identified goals or missions, which now became the re-emphasized school improvement process as projected by the research studies conducted by Hallinger, 2005.

This re-invigorated and continuously adaptive school improvement planning process was a key platform for instructional leaders to challenge the status quo, focus on innovation, and to collaborate with teachers on adapting mission statements, goals, and clarifying the instructional work that needed to be done. The new emerging and diverse delivery systems demanded by responses to the punctuated equilibrium fundamentally shook the foundations of the previous well-established traditional educational system.

However, instructional leaders began building the efficacy within teachers to create curriculum, instruction, and assessment opportunities for students that aligned with their futures based on the coherence framework four components: focused directions; cultivating collaborative cultures; securing accountability; and deepening learning. Skilled instructional leaders developed highly effective teams and built the capacity of each team member through the framework and components as previously envisioned in numerous school district strategic plans (Fullan & Kirtman, 2019, p. 48).

Referencing the coherence framework component of cultivating collaborative cultures teams of teachers and other stakeholders gained the efficacy to promote curriculum, instruction, and assessment opportunities and adaptions that were aligned with the "new" mission statements and school improvement goals.

One of the main ways that instructional leaders were effective during this crisis was due to the previous work done in school districts in creating professional learning communities (PLCs) made up of teachers, specialists, coaches, and administrators. PLC team members were prepared to focus on "revised" school improvement plans and started to collaborate on how to achieve success for students within their instructional purview during this crisis experience.

As stated by Fullan and Kirtman in *Coherent School Leadership: Forging Clarity from Complexity* (2019) . . . when leaders want people to be engaged and committed to the goals of the organization, they need to be part of the decision-making process and have genuine opportunities to lead." This was how PLCs throughout the United States built teacher efficacy and agency during the pandemic crisis.

PLC members worked together using their individual and group strengths to support the ever-changing curriculum and instructional goals of the school. When the PLCs were working effectively, the instructional leader needed to continue to cultivate and personally manage them to keep the engagement going (Fullan & Kirtman, 2019). This assured that the emerging collaboration and culture were aligned with the focus for curriculum, instruction, and assessments.

Key examples of the emerging collaborative culture of the COVID-19 pandemic were the extensive and intensive reliance in most school districts on virtual PLC meetings. Yet, the instructional leaders needed to make sure that these virtual PLCs were still focusing on curriculum, instruction, and assessment practices that aligned with the school's vision and mission in order to maintain fidelity to the educational expectations of the various school districts.

Securing accountability was also a major crisis responsibility of local instructional leaders working within the four components of the coherence framework. To secure accountability, instructional leaders needed to have assessment leadership skills that focused on framing assessment literacy for teachers and students. In addition, leaders needed to keep their local well informed about the assessment practices they would employ to evaluate student or program learning outcomes and academic progress.

The instructional leader's role during the crisis was to frame school goals that focus on their work with staff to ensure that instructional goals are clear, measurable, and time-based on academic progress (Hallinger, 2005). The instructional leader became the promoter for these goals and appropriately communicated them to school stakeholders to create a common assessment literacy for students, teachers, and parents at the classroom, program, and institutional accountability levels.

Throughout the COVID-19 global pandemic assessment leadership was, and continues to be, an important part of instructional leadership. During PLC collaborations on the new blended learning opportunities for students, the instructional leader needed to make sure assessments within these new formats aligned with intended learning outcomes (ILOs) and intended program outcomes (IPOs). A key dimension of assessment leadership was the need for instructional leaders to be engaged in the supervising and monitoring of teaching and learning in the school or district (Hallinger, 2005).

Instructional leaders needed to monitor PLCs to make sure that their work was focused on valid and reliable assessments that align with ILOs, especially within blended learning formats. These valid and reliable assessments should support and verify the learning (Stiggins & Duke, 2008). This was done with formative and summative assessments. The results of this focus on valid and reliable assessments confirmed the view that "when used effectively, as a teacher tool, classroom assessments have proven its ability to greatly enhance (not nearly monitor) ILOs (Stiggins & Duke, 2008, p. 288).

Not only did instructional leaders need to manage PLC work for ILOs, they also had to monitor intended program outcomes (IPOs). As districts ventured into blended learning experiences for students, instructional leaders needed to make sure that the educational programs set up to help teachers build efficacy with blended learning and/or to help students succeed in the "revised" school settings were being effective.

Historically, program-level assessments allowed teacher leaders, administrators, curriculum personnel, and others to evaluate a program's effectiveness and plan for implementation to help students learn (Stiggins & Duke, 2008, p. 286). Using formative assessments for program evaluation, like discussing needs and creating feedback loops with program stakeholders, helped build programs to be successful resources for student learning during the COVID-19 pandemic.

Multiple and diverse feedback loops like surveys or meetings with stakeholders were often used to consistently gain their input on how to improve educational programs during the unique experiences presented by navigating through the initial stages of this crisis turbulence.

Contemporary instructional leaders also needed to verify, as best as they could, that their students were prepared for their future work. GenZers, those individuals born between 1996–2010, are the first children born in a world of smart devices and the first students to be born After Google (AG) (Clark, 2019).

In a school environment, whether face to face, online, or blended, this implied that memorizing facts was not something students needed to master because Google, Alexa, and Siri already have this knowledge. Teachers needed to create deeper and more meaningful learning opportunities for students, especially given the realities of this instantaneous information digital age.

Deeper learning is the fourth component that instructional leaders needed to focus on when creating coherence within curriculum, instruction, and assessment. From the *Virginia is for Learning* website, the Virginia Department of Education (VDOE) has labeled these deeper learning skills as *The 5 C's: Communication, Collaboration, Citizenship, Critical Thinking, and Creative Thinking* (VDOE, 2019).

These five deeper learning skills represented what the VDOE listed as the key curriculum, instruction, and assessment needs for successful survival in the future and were referenced as the "Profile of a Virginia Graduate." It was up to instructional leaders to create efficacy and agency within teachers so that they became more innovative and continuously adaptive in using these skills to create deeper and meaningful learning experiences that are differentiated and personalized for students.

It was imperative for school instructional leaders to provide students educational experiences that helped them to initially survive and eventually thrive in a world "that values them for what they can do, not the facts they know" (Dintersmith & Wagner, 2016). This perspective was well within the context of blended learning experiences that educators typically created for students because of the COVID-19 pandemic because most instructional leaders had the courage and the mindset to advocate for innovation and adaption within curriculum, instruction, and assessments.

Being the spark for innovation of deeper and more meaningful learning experiences, effective instructional leaders involved all stakeholders to gain feedback and ideas. Successful leaders don't go with only like-minded innovators, they deliberately build in difference (Fullan, 2007, p. 42). Innovation is thinking differently, which means that instructional leaders needed to leverage all ideas about blended learning experiences and the possible immediate future to create deeper learning opportunities for students within instruction and assessment approaches.

Technology in schools needed to mirror this, and accordingly, facilitate the redefining of the teaching-learning process. Technology, should not have been viewed as a tool to replace human interaction during a crisis or at any time, but as an enabler for students and teachers to develop and exercise agency as they create or adapt the learning process with technology, not just consume it (Wilhoit, Pettenger, & Rickbaugh, 2016).

Providing the "Spark" for Instructional Changes During a Crisis

It is important for effective instructional leaders to create a culture of agency for learning in AG (After Google) contexts. "Leaders need to create a culture of producing the capacity to seek, critically assess, and selectively incorporate new ideas and practices" (Fullan, 2007, p. 44). Giving teachers the opportunity to create their own learning when navigating different uses of technology started to create a culture of capacity building and agency of learning in many school districts during this crisis.

Both teachers and students needed emergency type exposures to experiences that are unstructured, unfamiliar, and offered opportunities of choice that helped them to see themselves as leaders of themselves as well as others, thus creating agency of learning (Wilhoit, et al., 2016). As a result of experiences associated with instructing students during this crisis, teachers built their capacity to have agency for learning after being exposed to different experiences which created innovative ideas and adaptive practices for future face to face, online, and blended learning.

RESEARCH ON ADAPTING INSTRUCTION TO MEET STUDENT NEEDS AND INTERESTS VIA PLCS

Several contemporary research studies provide examples from diverse contextual settings to illustrate how educators, at all levels of the instructional spectrum, have a high degree of professional readiness and an acute personal eagerness to adapt their curriculum and instructional practices to accommodate the needs and interests of their students. Some may simply need a gentle "push" to do so while others may have needed strong leadership directions to make changes. But, a crisis may provide the "punctuation" necessary to make fundamental changes.

However, most educators needed additional focused reflection and guided direction from instructional leaders to spark significant adaptations to their traditional teaching and learning experiences to include more comprehensive student-centered constructivist practices such as greater differentiation of instruction approaches, strategies, and techniques (Eller et al., 2019; Polka, 2010; Polka et al., 2016).

Even the most experienced educators in various national survey samples identified that they needed a research-based theoretical framework about constructivist practices regarding current instructional practices as well as some acute specific examples in order to consider employing more differentiated learning experiences for their respective students. The survey instrument employed by the various research teams was designed to address both the theoretical needs and the pragmatic needs of teachers desirous of being more student-centered in their curriculum and instructional approaches (Polka, 2010).

The results of those studies conducted with practicing K–12 teachers by members of that *National Differentiating Instruction Team* for over a decade (Polka, et al., 2016), provided the pragmatic conceptual framework and key procedural guidelines for instructional leaders and administrators to employ with their Professional Learning Communities (PLC). This approach is consistent with professional learning team research that advocates analyzing appropriate adaptions of current teaching-learning experiences, based on best-practices and desired outcomes, in order to improve quality instruction for more students (Hersi & Bal, 2021).

The research studies about teacher discrepancies between their current level of differentiation of instruction practices compared to their desired level of employing such instructional practices were conducted and analyzed in the following fourteen states in diverse contexts including: Arkansas; Georgia; Idaho; Indiana; Kansas; Mississippi; Maryland; Missouri; New York; Ohio; South Carolina; South Dakota; Texas; and Virginia (Eller, et al., 2019; Hersi & Bal, 2021; Peace, et al., 2017; Polka, 2010; Polka et al., 2016).

Each respective research team utilized the same survey instrument titled, *Desired and Current Use of Constructivist Activities and Techniques* (See Appendix A) to capture the discrepancy data from practicing teachers regarding their *current use* and their *desired use* of instructional activities and techniques associated with individualized instruction and customized learning. The survey instrument consisted of twenty-five statements with Likert scale responses for both "desired use" and "actual use," consequently, the survey instrument enabled researchers to collect data for sample responses to a total of fifty statements.

The reliability of the instrument was previously determined using Cronbach's Alpha reliability test, accordingly, the twenty-five statements with the *desired use* focus had a reliability of $\alpha = 0.935$ and the twenty-five statements with the *actual use* focus had a reliability of $\alpha = 0.93$, yielding high reliability for both desired and actual responses (Polka, 2010). The construct validity of the twenty-five statements, categorized into nine categories of instructional behaviors are identified in Appendix B of this book for reader reference.

Accordingly, the twenty-five statements included in the survey instrument were divided into nine broad teaching-learning behavior categories, based on research at the University of Pittsburgh (Heathers, 1968), as follows: (1) Teacher Objectives, (2) Teaching Planning and Preparation, (3) Teacher Communication and Messages, (4) Teacher Behavior, (5) Student Objectives, (6) Student Planning and Preparation, (7) Classroom Expectations of Students, (8) Student Communication and Messages, and (9) Student Evaluations (Polka, 2010; Polka et al., 2016; Eller et al., 2019).

The nine teaching-learning behaviors are identified at the center between the two poles of the diagram, whereas specific activities associated with those behaviors are identified to the left of the teaching-centered pole and those specific activities associated with the learner-centered behaviors are identified to the right of that pole.

The Teaching-Learning Polarity Diagram

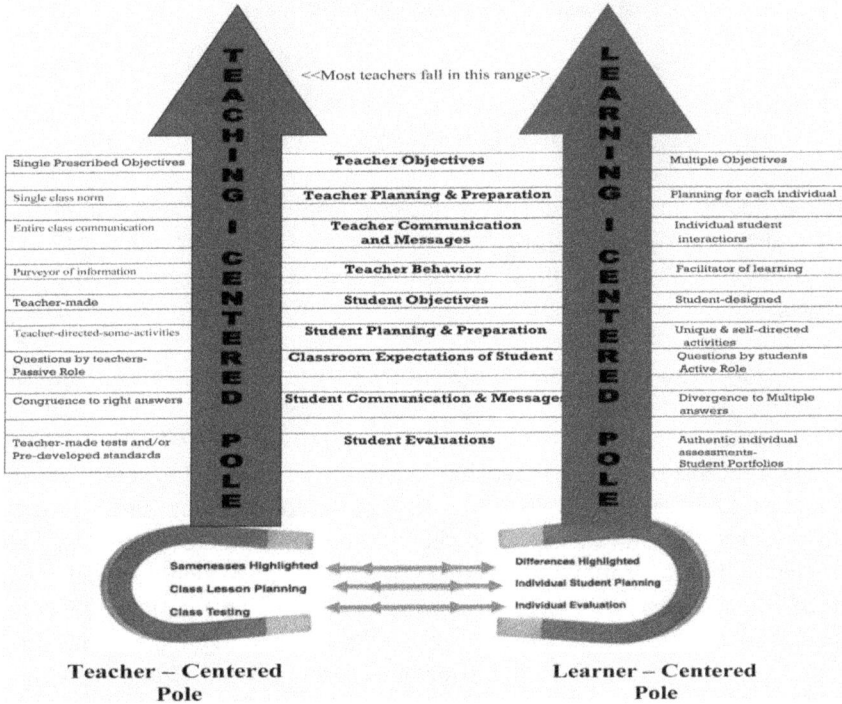

<<Most teachers fall in this range>>

Teacher – Centered Pole		Learner – Centered Pole
Single Prescribed Objectives	**Teacher Objectives**	Multiple Objectives
Single class norm	**Teacher Planning & Preparation**	Planning for each individual
Entire class communication	**Teacher Communication and Messages**	Individual student interactions
Purveyor of information	**Teacher Behavior**	Facilitator of learning
Teacher-made	**Student Objectives**	Student-designed
Teacher-directed-some-activities	**Student Planning & Preparation**	Unique & self-directed activities
Questions by teachers-Passive Role	**Classroom Expectations of Student**	Questions by students Active Role
Congruence to right answers	**Student Communication & Messages**	Divergence to Multiple answers
Teacher-made tests and/or Pre-developed standards	**Student Evaluations**	Authentic individual assessments-Student Portfolios

Samenesses Highlighted	Differences Highlighted
Class Lesson Planning	Individual Student Planning
Class Testing	Individual Evaluation

Teacher – Centered Pole **Learner – Centered Pole**

Figure 4.1 The Teaching-Learning Polarity Diagram
Polka, 2002

The above figure was designed to illustrate that the teacher-centered pole attracts teachers who practice traditional professional educator behaviors such as class lesson planning and whole class testing, whereas the learner-centered pole attracts teachers who practice constructivist professional educator behaviors such as individual student planning and individual evaluation.

Subsequently, the goal of the survey instrument was to facilitate professional learning communities (PLCs) in various micro (school) and macro (district) settings to establish collaborative experiences wherein instructional leaders would facilitate teacher self-reflections of their practice. Subsequently, individual teachers and teams of teachers would analyze their instructional practices in terms of those two competing poles of teaching-learning behaviors and determine where they would like to be and how to get there.

Instructional leaders at the school, district, or regional level would then be tasked to review and analyze the activities that various teachers have used to move their own professional practices to the desired state of student-centered instruction, if that was the vision for the school, and consider how those activities may be adapted by others into their respective teaching-learning situations in the least personally stressful fashion.

RESULTS OF THE DIFFERENTIATION SURVEY STUDIES AND IMPLICATIONS FOR INSTRUCTIONAL LEADERS

The collected and analyzed data from over 1,500 teachers who completed the survey instrument and had opportunities to review their individual and team results in Professional Learning Community settings provided valuable benchmarks to determining the best approaches to facilitate greater differentiation of instruction in diverse contexts.

Those aggregated benchmarks may prove very useful to other instructional leaders considering major changes in teaching-learning behaviors based on the experiences associated with crisis situations like COVID-19. The benchmarks from this longitudinal national study may be used as key references in implementing fundamental long-term changes in the teaching learning paradigm such as the movement to blended or virtual learning for more students.

The following information includes the generalized responses in category three. The category with major discrepancies between the desired practices of teachers and their actual level of practice related to differentiation of instruction. It severs as a model for instructional leaders contemplating working with PLCs to determine the post-crisis "best fit" curriculum and instruction options for their schools and school districts.

In category four, the aggregated survey statement benchmarks with the greatest discrepancy between desired practice and actual practice are also specifically identified. This information has been provided to encourage instructional leaders within the PLCs to identify the constructivist practices that must be addressed to move more teachers to the learner-centered pole of instruction. However, it may take more time and resources to accomplish this move because the discrepancies are so significant.

Category Three Discrepancy-Major Differences Between Desired Practice and Actual Practice

At this step, instructional leaders were encouraged to help the faculty reflect about what they currently do by providing specific examples of how they incorporate some of the following constructivist activities in their respective courses and how they can do more to master the incorporation of these practices in their current instructional programs given some additional support and assistance:

- Diagnostic elements, such as IQ, reading level, and math ability, are used to plan individual student activities.
- Knowledge of each student including life outside of school is used to plan instructional activities.
- The students and teacher respect the diverse opinions of others and come to agreements in a collegial fashion.
- Pretests and other similar diagnostic instruments are used to determine the parts of a unit that individual students need.
- Students conduct a major part of their learning on a self-directed basis.
- Lesson planning is done for individual students rather than for the entire class.

Since the above constructivist strategies and techniques are discrepant at the third quartile level according to study samples, then the instructional leader should focus professional development on practicing teachers working together with other faculty members to investigate ways to incorporate more of these strategies and techniques into their instruction.

However, instructional leaders are cautioned to modify and adjust this process according to the needs and acceptance levels of the faculty. The process for the faculty itself must be customized and differentiated.

Category Four Discrepancy-Greatest Differences Between Desired Practice and Actual Practice

At this step, instructional leaders are encouraged to help the faculty reflect about what they have done or observed others doing related to the identified statements of this category's constructivist activities. It is also imperative for leaders to facilitate faculty comprehensive awareness and provide pragmatic illustrations of the following student-centered practices in current instructional programs by providing additional professional training, research, and assistance related to them:

- Sufficient time is allocated for students to think, play with ideas, manipulate objects, and experiment in learning without pressure to get "the right answer" at the "right time."
- The time that students have to complete or master a given concept or skill varies based on individual differences.
- Student evaluations are based on individual learning growth instead of a fixed standard all are expected to learn.
- Students are evaluated individually and move on to another task once they have mastered the objectives on a unit.

- Students play an active role of contributing to the direction or content of the lessons in their learning experiences.

Instructional leaders must focus on facilitating authentic faculty collaborations as well as providing additional professional development related to such constructivism approaches as identified above so as to promote meaningful reflections and pragmatic actions about how to incorporate more of these strategies and techniques into the desired "new normal" teaching-learning settings of the post-crisis period.

Making changes to promote greater congruence between desired practice and actual practice at this level will take more time, energy, and resources since the above practices have been identified as being the instructional statements from the national survey instrument with the greatest discrepancy between desired practice and actual practice (Polka et al., 2016). However, the approaches used by instructional leaders with their PLCs to promulgate such a major change must themselves be customized and differentiated consistent with constructivism beliefs.

In addition, members of the different research teams associated with this national study contend that the most effective way to promote more student-centered learning or differentiation at any level of the instructional spectrum pre-K through 12 is to employ a progressive but cautious reflective approach to major instructional changes which includes going only as "fast as possible" but as "slow as necessary" when working with the professional staff since at this level such a significant change in teacher-student behaviors from current practices.

It is recommended that instructional leaders working with their respective PLCs incorporate the key concepts and procedures employed in these differentiation of instruction studies to make long-range significant innovations in their schools' instructional programs based on the expedited teaching-learning experiences associated with COVID-19, especially given the widespread use of technology in education and resultant attractions to more virtual and blended education.

Instructional leaders should start the process using examples of various COVID-19 crisis teaching-learning strategies, techniques, and specific activities employed by teachers within their PLCs and provide opportunities for the teachers to reflect about both their successes using them as well as the obstacles that they encountered during their time teaching during the crisis.

This is a valuable approach for instructional leaders to employ with their PLCs as it also develops professional respect and pragmatic learnings that should result in a greater acceptance of diverse techniques and strategies to adapt for virtual or blended instructional settings. The global pandemic crisis was a major punctuation to the traditional teaching and learning approaches and has provided instructional leaders with a unique opportunity to further advance more student-centered learning programs than previously possible.

Thus, the research studies presented in this section of the chapter provide benchmarks and procedures based on comprehensive research from diverse contextual settings to illustrate teachers, at all levels of the instructional spectrum, currently employ some key student-centered approaches but professionally desire to learn how to employ more.

However, they need instructional leaders who provide the additional focused and guided reflection opportunities regarding current instructional practices as well as acute examples of "best fit" practices in their local contexts in order to help them consider employing more.

When professionally interacting with individual teachers, teams of teachers, or PLCs, effective instructional leaders must possess the courage and intentional orientation "to take them . . . where they don't necessarily want to go, but ought to be." The results of the various studies associated with the identified national study of differentiation provide valuable practical guidelines to do so.

These guidelines and the self-reflective survey instrument identified above may be replicated by instructional leaders who are working with PLCs to plan for the post-crisis realities of education that probably will include more blended and virtual learning settings.

FINAL THOUGHTS

Leading change is complex, and in times of extensive turbulence even more challenging, but effective instructional leaders understand that a coherent system of curriculum, instruction, and assessment is always needed to make sure students are given equitable opportunities to learn no matter the delivery format employed. As stated by Ralph Waldo Emerson "What lies behind you and what lies in front of you, pales in comparison to what lies inside you," this holds true for instructional leaders.

Subsequently, instructional leaders need the internal courage to spark innovations for deeper learning experiences for all students in unprecedented times of crisis and change while maintaining coherence in curriculum, instruction, and assessment. The traditional delivery systems of education were challenged by the unexpected punctuated equilibrium COVID-19 experiences and will continue to be challenged in the "new normal" climate of education because some of the changes enacted to confront seemingly uncontrollable external forces resulted in different but still successful teaching-learning experiences.

The task ahead for instructional leaders is to identify the teaching-learning settings, curriculum strategies, and techniques, as well as, specific instructional activities and materials that worked well for most teachers and learners during the crisis in their respective contexts and to emphasize the value of some of those changes for improving education in the post-crisis period.

Once identified, just like in the differentiation studies referenced above, instructional leaders can work with individual teachers and PLCs to ferret out those strategies and techniques that worked best and were most readily accepted and adapted by the faculty. They can then proceed to facilitate teacher reflections about the *desired state* for instruction in their "new normal" local educational system and plan how best to get there based on the *actual state* for most teachers. It will not be an easy task since there is always a tendency to "return to tradition" and the perceived teaching-learning homeostasis of the past.

However, this crisis has become the harbinger of fundamental changes and a "new normal" in education in terms of teaching and learning. Instructional leaders must capitalize on this opportunity to promote curriculum and instructional adaptations so that the educational system evolves and continues to survive. It is imperative that instructional leaders possess the creativity, focus, and fortitude to appropriately be the sparks for meaningful deeper learning changes and be the astute pilots, as Twain described, to help others effectively navigate through any turbulence.

KEY PRAGMATIC LEADERSHIP
TAKEAWAYS FROM CHAPTER 4

- *Instructional leaders must have an adaptable vision for teaching and learning, but also, need to have focus, be creative, and have fortitude.* They must have the intense desire to lead and take control of the people, things, and ideas of their micro context, especially in crisis situations. And, they must be ready to "take people where they don't necessarily want to go, but ought to be" based on their analysis of the exigencies of their contexts including during the crisis and in the post-crisis period.
- *Instructional leaders possess an unbridled passion for teaching and learning and always wear their love for it on their sleeves, figuratively, no matter the title of their office.* The have an unquenchable desire to be like Mr. Chips, spending their entire career enthusiastically teaching, learning, and serving as role models for others. They believe in that saying, "The wise person controls their destiny . . . but, education points the way." Thus, they must have a "perpetual obsession" to improve instruction for all and show it in their actions and decisions as leaders.

Leaders must recognize that the supervision of people, things, and ideas in their organization is a 24/7 responsibility. They need to recognize that educational leaders—paraphrasing Mark Twain—"need to know more than any one leader ought to be allowed to know and that they must learn it all over again in a different way every 24 hours" in order to survive and thrive during crises situations and in post-crisis settings.

- *Instructional leaders must keep ubiquitously current and acutely aware of their respective micro and macro-organizational contexts as well as the mega landscape environment.* They need to recognize that change, whether man-made or natural, never sleeps!

- *Effective instructional leaders understand that a coherent system of curriculum, instruction, and assessment is always needed to make sure students are given equitable opportunities to learn no matter the delivery format employed.* Instructional leaders need to be prepared to adapt their micro-contextual professional development activities and PLC programs to address changes in the macro-contextual state or national educational standards and expectations for student learning.

- *Instructional leaders must be personally and professionally efficacious and continuously serve "educational concierges" to their followers pointing the way to deeper and more meaningful learnings and facilitating the development their efficacy and agency propensities* (Pearman, C., et al, 2021; Polka, W., et al, 2017; Polka, W. & Rudolph, A., 2021). They must internalize that Emerson quote and aggressively promote it to others, that no matter the circumstances of your personal and professional journey, "What lies behind you and what lies in front of you, pales in comparison to what lies inside you."

- *Instructional leaders need to employ specific research-based models for changing the teaching-learning paradigm in their context and empower others to comfortably demonstrate their actual practices in becoming more student-centered during both normal times or times of crisis.* Instructional leaders should review the research and procedures associated with the various differentiation of instruction studies (Eller, et al., 2019; Hersi & Bal, 2021; Peace, et al., 2017; Polka, 2010; Polka et al., 2016).

- *Instructional leaders may wish to replicate those differentiation of instruction studies using the existing survey instrument (see Appendix A) or modifying the instrument as appropriate.* Using that survey instrument and the recommended approaches would effectively measure the current teaching-learning behavior changes provoked by the COVID-19 crisis in their respective contexts.

Subsequently, the implementation strategies to achieve the desired long-term benefits of those changes for both teachers and students could be identified.

- *Instructional leaders need to recognize and continuously promote the significance of that quote originally attributed to Charles Darwin,* "It is not the strongest of the species that survives, nor the most intelligent. . . . It is the one that is the most adaptable to change. Changes in education will always occur—sometimes quickly (as a punctuated equilibrium crisis) or slowly—and those leaders who are most adaptable will survive and thrive. So, as an instructional leader, always be sure that your "adaptability quotient" is higher than your "strength quotient" or your "intelligence quotient"!

REFERENCES

Aspen Education & Society Program (2017). *Leading for equity: Opportunities for state education chiefs.* Washington, DC: Council of Chief State School Officers.

Clark, H. (2019). *Teachers meet generation z.* Retrieved from http://www.hollyclark .org/2019/04/30/teachers-meet-generation-z/

Constantino, S. & Staples, S. (2019). *Profile of a Virginia graduate.*[PowerPoint Slides]. Retrieved from William and Mary's EPPL 501 Educational Leadership Course Session 5 Deeper Learning.

Dinthersmith, T. & Wagner, T. (2016). *Most likely to succeed: Preparing our kids for the innovation era.* New York, New York: Simon & Schuster Inc.

Eller, A., Polka, W., & Young, W. (2019). Planning for increased differentiation via focused teacher reflections about desired constructivist practices and current realities. *Educational Research: Theory and Practice,* 30(1), 7–18.

Emerson, R. (n.d). Retrieved May 24, 2020 from https://www.brainyquote.com/ authors/ralph-waldo-emerson-quotes

Fullan, M. (2007). *Leading in a culture of change.* San Francisco, CA: Wiley & Sons, Incorporated. 15–122.

Fullan, M. & Kirtman, L. (2019) *Coherent school leadership: Forging clarity from complexity.* Alexandria, VA: ASCD.

Gareis, C. (2020). *Program evaluation: An introduction for assessment leaders.* [Powerpoint Slides]. Retrieved from William and Mary's EPPL 535 Instructional Leadership: Assessment and Evaluation Course Session 7 Assessment Systems & Program Evaluation.

Gareis, C. & Grant, L. (2015). *Teacher-made assessments: How to connect curriculum, instruction, and student learning (2nd Edition).* New York, NY: Taylor & Francis.

Hallinger, P. (2005). Instructional leadership and the school principal: A passing fancy that refuses to fade away. *Leadership and Policy in Schools,* 4, 221–239. https://doi .org/10.1080/15700760500244793

Hersi, A. & Bal, I. (2021) Planning for differentiation: Understanding Maryland teachers' desired and actual use of differentiated instruction. *Educational Planning* 28(1), 55–72.

Krueger, N. (2014). *3 Critical mindsets for blended learning.* ISTE.org. Retrieved May 24, 2020, from https://www.iste.org/explore/ISTE-blog/3-critical-mindsets-for-blended-learning

Marzano, R (2003). *What works in schools: Translating research into action.* Alexandria, VA: ASCD. 22–34.

Merriam-Webster. (n.d.). Punctuated equilibrium. In *Merriam-Webster.com dictionary.* Retrieved May 24, 2020, from https://www.merriamwebster.com/dictionary/punctuated%20equilibrium

Peace, T., Polka, W., & Mete, R. (2017). Assessing and promoting student-centered teaching and learning practices using a quantitative educational planning tool: Results of 2016 Indiana case study. *Educational Planning.* 24(2), 21–37.

Pearman, C., Bowles, F., & Polka, W. (2021). Teacher educator perceptions of characteristics of self-efficacy. *Critical Questions in Education,* 12(1), 80–96.

Polka, W. (2002). Facilitating the transition from teacher centered to student-centered instruction at the university level via constructivist principles and customized learning plans. *Educational Planning,* 13(3), 55–61.

Polka, W. (2010). The art and science of constructivist supervision: Transforming schools by applying needs-based research. *Journal for the Practical Application of Constructivist Theory in Education,* 5(1), 1–28.

Polka, W., Fernandes, A., Smith, E., & Flynn, K. (2017). Challenge: Efficacious teachers view obstacles as opportunities. In F. Bowles and C. Pearman (Eds.). *Self-efficacy in action: Tales from the classroom for teaching, learning, and professional development.* Lanham, Maryland: Rowman & Littlefield (57–68).

Polka, W. & Rudolph, A. (2021). Efficacy and Agency. In F. Fulton, J. Yoshioka, & N. Gallavan (Eds). *Online teaching and learning for teacher educators.* Lanham, Maryland: Rowman & Littlefield (111–122).

Polka, W. & VanHusen, M. (2014). Applying teacher reflection strategies to promote greater differentiation of instruction: A practical research model and procedural guide. In E. E., Pultorak (Ed.). *Reflectivity and cultivating student learning: Critical elements for enhancing a global community of learners and educators.* Lanham, Maryland: Rowman & Littlefield (111–135).

Polka, W., VanHusen, M., Young, W., & Minervino, K. (2016). Facilitating greater instructional differentiation via research-based teacher reflections and site-based procedural guidelines. *Educational Research: Theory & Practice,* 28(1), 37–52.

Schmoker, M. (2011). *Focus: Evaluating the essentials to radically improve student learning.* Alexandria, VA: ASCD. 9–49.

Stiggins, R. & Duke, D. (2008). Effective instructional leadership requires assessment leadership. *Phi Delta Kappan, 90*(4), 285–291.

Twain, M. (1886) *Life on the Mississippi.* Germany: Jazzybee Verlag. Retrieved May 24, 2020 from https://www.google.com/books/edition/_/zpBBDwAAQBAJ?hl=en

VanHusen, M. (2019). *Advice for a gen z school leader* (Personal Correspondence). Department of Educational Leadership, University of William and Mary.

VanHusen, M. (2020). *A framework, self-evaluation, & professional develop-ment plan for assessment leadership* (Personal Correspondence). Department of Educational Leadership, University of William and Mary.

Virginia Department of Education. The 5C's. (2019). Retrieved from www.virginiaisforlearners.virginia.gov

Wilhoit, G., Pittenger, L., & Rickbaugh, J. (2016). *Leadership for learning: What is leadership's role in supporting success for every student?* Lexington, KY: Center for Innovation in Education.

Chapter 5

Managing the Auxiliary School Services

Budget, Finances, Facilities, Transportation, and Food Services in Crisis Situations

Rubie Harris

This chapter illuminates the myriad experiences of an assistant superintendent for school business and finance and the various trials and tribulations of maintaining the business of the school district during the pandemic, including food services for students, facilities maintenance, budget appropriations, and financial investments.

It should be noted that the author of this chapter is the assistant superintendent for business and finance of the school district used as the case study in this chapter. She is relatively new to the position of assistant superintendent for business and finance in this medium-sized, suburban school district, as she was appointed only months prior to the start of the pandemic crisis.

However, the author of this chapter had previous experiences in other similar districts, including: a small city school district for four years as an administrator, and four years in the business office of a larger city school district. In addition, she is a certified New York school district business administrator, having completed education degrees focused on school business management, including a BS, an MBA Advanced Certification Degree of School District Business Leader, and a PhD in leadership and policy in 2017. The title of her PhD dissertation is: A *mixed-methods exploration of the financial planning of New York State school districts with a negative tax cap compliance scenario.*

She poignantly remembers those initial experiences she had enjoying learning about the general culture and business procedures of the suburban New
York school where she was just beginning her new role as assistant superintendent for business and finance when the COVID-19 punctuated equilibrium
crisis began in March of 2020. The following are her accounts and reflections
through her school business official lens of this unique experience.

THAT FIRST DAY: FACING THE FIVE
FS OF AUXILIARY SERVICES

It was Sunday, March 15 at 11:30 a.m., and a meeting was being held with the
superintendent and cabinet-level administrators to discuss the meal waiver
submission and the possibility of schools closing within the coming days and
weeks. The chapter leadership of the Association of School Business Officials
had met days prior in Albany about budget initiatives, where a discussion of
COVID-19 spread quickly and took over the meeting objectives at large.

Many of hypothesized about the next courses of action that could be taken
if schools were to close. Some even began to predict possible executive
orders from the governor. Within an hour of that initial discussion, a letter
was composed and "blasted" out to the community, using multiple channels
of communications as schools in multiple counties of New York state pulled
the plug and decided to close.

The decision to close schools caused a cascade of questions: What should
we do now to manage the myriad aspects of schooling in local communities,
and how long will school leaders be able to manage this crisis, as it appeared
everyone was "flying by the seat of our pants?"

When the school district superintendent sent that closing message, the initial thoughts of many school leaders first was one of anxiety regarding what
happens now and the next steps for the immediate future. The following are
the types of questions that circulated among all of the key district administrators responsible for directing various aspects school district operations: What
were the next steps to be taken with staff, and how long would this crisis last?

A significant concern, expressed by district leaders in school districts
with multiple school sites, was: What if schools would open again for the
remainder of the 2019–2021 school year and there were multiple confirmed
COVID-19 cases among students, staff, and community members would that
require multiple future shutdowns and re-openings?

However, the district leadership team began to quickly identify the major
priorities at this moment such as: making sure students were fed, providing
students with the proper technology to be taught from home, and any information control with the union and staff in terms of what was coming within

the days and months ahead and what would be their roles and responsibilities. District leaders began contacting the union representatives and other administrators to get a handle on what should and should not be communicated at the current time.

The assistant superintendent for business and finance was charged with sending the building level leaders a message of what information related to the crisis to share and when they would receive an update from the superintendent so they would know how to proceed. When placed under this level of pressure, trained leaders like other humans, often times become unsure of how to appropriately respond, so it was essential for the district executive leadership team to get in front of communication coming from all leadership groups within the district.

Initially, it was believed the shutdown would be for a couple of weeks; it was not yet understood that this COVID-19 crisis would turn into a full global pandemic. Within a week, it was necessary for all of the school district leaders to determine not only how to educate students but still operate as a business remotely. COVID-19 brought these five Fs to managing the auxiliary services in a school district to the forefront for those in the school district business and financial office and others in similar central office positions throughout New York: finances, facilities, food service, flexibility, and most importantly, future adjustments/moving forward.

These five Fs are things school business and financial leaders navigate daily. However, during a crisis, the pressure is on to not only determine the best approaches to deliver services but do it quickly and do it while the guidance from county, state, and federal officials is changing daytoday. This quixotic leadership experience is best reflected in Mark Twain's 1886 quote, cited in earlier chapters of this book:

> Two things seemed pretty apparent to me. One was that in order to be a Mississippi River pilot, a man had got to learn more than any one man ought to be allowed to know, and the other was that he must learn it all over again in a different way every 24 hours.

Yes, indeed, it became rapidly apparent to members of the district executive leadership team that each leader would be responsible for charting the course of their areas of responsibility of this school district during this punctuated equilibrium. Everyone recognized that each of them would need to learn more than any one man or woman ought to know about navigating through this turbulent time in our history. Not only that, but each would need to learn it all over again in a different way every twenty-four hours, as exemplified by the personal and professional experiences that follow.

Food Service

As mentioned above, New York school districts received executive orders requiring districts to provide meals throughout the pandemic, even though students were receiving distance learning from home. The student population of the school district highlighted in this chapter consists of about 2,800 K–12 students, and the general fund budget is around $64 million annually.

When you think about a district that size or larger, there is much thought that goes into the logistics of feeding all children and ensuring equal opportunity and access to breakfast and lunch for students. By week three of the closing of schools, many districts had developed a plan that allowed meal production on Monday, Wednesday, and Friday. They were producing thousands of meals per week to make sure students had enough breakfast and lunch throughout the week.

The assistant superintendent in this school district felt that it was imperative that school systems continue to provide one of their custodial expectations in their respective communities by providing for those basic Maslow Hierarchy Needs early and often during this pandemic. This caused a significant shift in the leader's thinking about school food services and their delivery during a pandemic, as well as a significant paradigm shift in thinking about providing for food needs of staff and the community in general.

Some districts provided the option to not only pick the meals up through a drive-through type setup but also arranged for drop-offs of meals through the district's transportation department or contracted transportation services. The assistant superintendent in this district stated, " . . . OMG, we were turning into an academic McDonald's or Burger King!"

People went from seeing and driving kids daily to school, to working on food assembly lines and becoming a delivery service very quickly with little to no complaints because we all felt that we needed to work together to survive in this new context. Districts utilized services such as email blasts and robocall for communicating to the community about the foodservice meal options, signup sheets occurred, and food service departments planned for the unknown of someone just showing up and requesting a meal so every student in need could have food.

Several school leaders expressed that they were summarily impressed by the focus and due diligence of school food service teams. Those food service teams responded to this call to provide these essential food school services to our students most efficiently and effectively. In this district those teams transformed into well-organized teams whose mission was of paramount importance to many of our students and their families.

Observing how people adjusted schedules, worked around shifts, and worked more hours to make sure every child was provided the opportunity for a meal was truly astonishing. It definitely illustrated the caring attitude of all district employees and their unbridled willingness to help students succeed and thrive in spite of the crisis.

A new school food preparation and distribution direction was provided before the scheduled spring break in 2020, which was canceled for many administrators and teachers so they could develop additional plans for providing needed educational services to our students. COVID-19 not only stopped people from the possibility of traveling, but also, through executive orders, required teachers to provide instruction. Meal services were continued during the break period.

School districts were required to provide a plan to the New York state education department regarding procedures designed to reach our high-poverty areas. In addition, clear communications were continuously presented to families throughout the community about the food service program and other opportunities. However, it was also necessary to develop accountability plans that incorporated the hours of operation and kept records of the students receiving meals during the COVID-19 pandemic.

This directive was frustrating when first received. It not only reflected an academic shift (teacher and student calendar impact) but also a financial impact. Food service employees are traditionally ten-month employees and do not receive wages during breaks, so this directive increased the expense area for food service to comply.

There was an initial concerned that staff who was already essential to come in throughout the closing would possibly refuse to work since it was not their regular time and they would usually be off for that week. In the end, the staff came to work, and a game plan was developed that worked well and still allowed them to enjoy a couple of days off for the break.

Facilities

At the same time that district executive leaders, like assistant superintendents, were navigating through the pandemic, ensuring each student had access to school breakfast and lunch, they were also working through the facilities' operations side of school business.

Upon the closing of all New York schools, districts were charged with cleaning and sanitizing every surface of every school district building. Though schools were closed to students, some school districts had staff reporting to create packets, provide instructional materials or technology, and clean out classrooms.

Student information and supplies preparation was occurring while the cleaning, maintenance, and custodial staff were sanitizing the building to lower the risk of exposure. The process of having the buildings accessible and keeping up with the cleaning standard, while upholding the order that people should gather in groups of less than ten was very trying at times for the managers.

The added thoughts of moving forward and ensuring that buildings are kept up to recommended cleaning standards became overwhelming for some individuals, but again, the team effort was incredible as everyone became unselfishly engaged in continuously working to provide safe environments for all.

The district had to purchase supplies and materials that were approved by the Centers for Disease Control and Prevention at the level advised to sanitize the buildings. Some of them were difficult, if not impossible, to purchase because of the limited supplies and high demand throughout the state and region.

The executive order that required building staff reductions due to "safe-distancing practices" while districts attempted to keep up with the sanitation and cleaning of buildings further complicated this cleaning process. The cut in staff left many charged to do more, with fewer employees in buildings.

The executive order from the governor's office that further reduced group sizes from one hundred people to fifty people, to then ten people or less within so many square feet, further exacerbated the situation. Districts were now in a position to hold meetings online, reduce cleaning and custodial staff, divide shifts, and allow clerical staff to work remotely unless coming into the office was necessary for things like mail pickup, bill payments, and payroll check printing.

During this time, district officials were faced with many complex problems to resolve about the people, things, and ideas associated with running the various dimensions of their educational operations. Leaders often felt overwhelmed by the number of questions that developed daily. Several of them identified that too often they felt that solving one problem resulted in creating new problems in addition to receiving ten more possible issues, per new directives from Albany or Washington.

Central office administrators became even more appreciative of the remarkable group of highly dedicated administrators and caring staff that continued to do their respective tasks at the building level. Their flexibility in dealing with numerous different directives and policy changes as well as their resolute willingness to come to the table with suggestions in how crisis operations could be effectively and efficiently improved with a reduced population of staff working.

Building access changed drastically as the crisis wore on in the spring of 2020, and it was mandatory to inform custodial staff if someone would be occupying the buildings, so they could daily make sure they cleaned areas that people had used. The notification of building usage allowed the district to reduce/eliminate the possibility of others coming in contact with the virus.

Board meetings moved out of the school district buildings into a virtual world, where district leadership worked on ways to provide for public comments and livestreaming and still provide safety and control to conduct the meeting properly. Perhaps some of these new modifications to our previous business facilities usage modus operandi are valuable to keep in mind for the future when there is a return to some type of "normalcy" in schools.

Perhaps COVID-19 has provided educational leaders at both the district and the building levels that many things are possible virtually and can assist not only with health and safety but also have financial savings in the areas of building operation hours, late board meetings, and so on. Several leaders in this school district commented that having digital capabilities allowed for all to be in attendance at required meetings. In addition, it enabled working from home to take place in the more often and more effectively than previously envisioned.

Finances

The COVID-19 crisis had a substantial impact on school districts, but it is crucial to identify that this pandemic broke during one of the most hectic financial planning times for school districts. March and April is the time that most school district financial leaders are finalizing their budgets and preparing to present them to the board for approval and to their community for final vote, but the pandemic crisis knocked that completely off-kilter.

There was no emergency plan for school districts to receive their anticipated state aid allocations for the current school year or to plan effectively for the next school year. There was no way to determine the net impact that this crisis was having on the general, state, and local economy. New York was in financial hardship, and all areas supported by funding from the State were going to experience a short-fall.

The unknown makes it near impossible to plan for the upcoming year when state aid, sales tax, and property taxes are all uncertain. Nevertheless, the financial leadership of the district did what anyone in similar administrative positions has always done, put together several scenarios with related plan based on funding stream probabilities.

The worst case scenario that was posited consisted of a possible 20 percent reduction in foundation aid and up to 90 percent reduction in sales tax revenue. If this were to occur in a district like the one of this case study, it would mean over a $5 million reduction in the general fund after the initial budget had been approved and adopted.

Though most districts have money available through fund balance and reserves, covering this type of gap is nearly impossible and would require a massive reduction in programs and staff. The preferred plan that emerged in this district was that there would be no reductions in the financial categories of foundation aid and sales tax, and that the budget could function as planned and provide students with all that is needed for the upcoming school year.

However, the most probable plan that was generally implemented by school financial leaders throughout the state consisted of a pandemic adjustment reduction plan, which was backfilled with the Federal CARES restoration that was provided to school districts for the 2020–21 school aid runs.

This enabled districts to recoup the amount of revenue in Foundational Aid that was initially reduced for each school district. This adjustment ranges from $100,000 to millions of dollars for districts throughout New York. This specific school district would lose almost $500,000. Though this is not preferred, it is manageable and a better scenario than the loss of 20 percent of foundation aid.

While attempting to get through the current year and plan for the upcoming year, the office of the assistant superintendent for business and finance was also tasked with providing absentee ballots for every registered voter that resides within the school district's limits. The changes made to the local school district voter participation program because of this global voter participation ranged from 15,000 to more than 100,000 absentee ballots being created, stuffed, and sent to every registered voter's home.

It also required districts to provide a return postage envelope for these ballots to be mailed back to schools to be counted to record a pass or fail budget for the 2020–21 school year. The cost of these accommodations was an added expense of $20,000 to more than $100,000 to school districts that were, of course, not budgeted nor planned.

Absentee ballots' disbursement added a high level of concern because most districts receive a minimal turnout for school budget votes. Each district now was faced with receiving 5 to 10 times greater the number of voter ballots through the absentee process. Absentee ballots increase the possibility of a budget failing, meaning that the school district's Board of Education may not be able to increase the tax levy and would have to make budgetary reductions to balance the budget for the upcoming school year.

This possibility was a compiling concern during a time of revenue uncertainty from the state and local levels. It could mean increasing class sizes, reducing staff and services, and removing opportunities that have taken years to put into place for students.

School business administrators throughout New York felt this was an interesting dilemma because they generally believe in the yearly democratic process conducted in New York School Districts regarding budget votes and elections to the Board of Education. However, they also recognize that many of the voters during this time may not have all of the necessary knowledge about the school budget to make informed decisions, and consequently, may vote more negatively than positively just because they can.

And, New York officials just made it easier for them to do so! Obviously, using these absentee ballots during the crisis increased the levels of stress during an already heighten period of anxiety related to the business and financial operations of schools.

Flexibility

One thing that COVID-19 produced was a need for organizational flexibility. "The goal of organizational flexibility is to enable the organization as a whole to adapt to rapidly changing demands placed on the organization from either internal or external forces" (Hill et al., 2008).

This level of flexibility was not merely a choice but very much a necessity for all school districts to discover and practice. This crisis made what seemed impossible, become a reality for many school districts. A majority of the staff were required to work from home, develop new office spaces, and still perform their daily functions needed in their job area. And, school administrators still needed to supervise and evaluate them!

As previously identified using that Mark Twain quote from 1886, the operations plans of action often changed, sometimes daily at the onset of the crisis, and sometimes weekly as the business and finance staff worked cooperatively with their educational leader to develop new procedures to deal with uncertainty.

Very often, the plans of engagement with all district stakeholders, especially with employees, students and parents changed as the governor's executive orders and local administrative decisions shifted and adjusted to the changing national and global situations. Subsequently, all departments, faculty, and staff had to adjust to those changes in such a quixotic environment and they needed to do it expediently and with due diligence!

Consequently, everything changed to a "new modus operandi" from virtual meetings, accessing financial systems from home, processing purchasing, payroll, and human resources functions from home and complete it in a timely manner. Forcing faculty and staff to use technology, whereas prior, they may not have felt comfortable in doing so.

The school district leaders provided employees with anything they needed to do their job differently due to the crisis including: frontline required training courses for cleaners and bus drivers to saving all documents to Google Drive so files are accessible for all staff at home. Things changed within days, and a lack of flexibility would hinder everyone in the educational field.

Perhaps this new, much more flexible mindset is another good aspect of this global pandemic. It required educational leaders to develop multiple contingency plans within their respective spheres of operations and also required faculty and support staff to engage with each other more often using "high-tech" formats and devices while still maintaining some key "high-touch" personal type interactions.

This flexible mindset is one that is currently referenced often as the plans for the future of education in this school district are discussed. School district administrators have evolved their operations to include having online video meetings and allowing for those who are comfortable to come into the buildings to meet as the strategic next steps of future planning.

The Future is for Moving Forward and Watching for the Next Crisis

The one question that everyone has asked and continues to ask of central office business administrators is: What happens next? What does the future hold for public education, and how do we move forward? Predicting what the future holds is one of the hardest parts of any situation you face and has amplified during a pandemic and exemplified the specific previous events articulated in this chapter.

Working through the logistics of what the eventual return of students, faculty, and school support staff will look like during and immediate post-pandemic era while still abiding by the social distancing guidelines of six feet of separation and personal masking is something challenging to continually imagine. However, it is something that should constantly be in the mindset of school leaders so that viable tactical and strategic plans for our new future,

Buses that usually transport forty to sixty students in one run may only carry twenty to thirty students. Classrooms that provide educational resources to twenty to twenty-five students at one time are now facing reductions. School business officials often reflect on these thoughts of our near future since they are thoughts within the purview as the school business official's role to operationalize and administrate them effectively.

However, most school business officials are increasingly anxious about how do it. But, most possess a very confident attitude that cooperatively school personnel and community members together can make it happen for the good of our school district and the education of our students.

Lunchrooms that allowed a couple of hundred students to unite at one time will, in the future, possibly occur in classrooms. Contractual obligations between districts and unions will have to be adjusted to allow for student supervision due to the possibility of classroom changes promulgated by safe distancing rules and regulations.

Building administrators will need to provide arrows to comply with social distancing guidelines and assist with student passing times as well as modify contractual provisions currently in place regarding faculty supervision of students.

Distance learning may still occur for the secondary grade levels to allow the elementary levels to divide the classroom space that now would become more available to educate daily. Offices will require partitions to divide desks, and all staff and students will need facial masks and will have to wear them for six to eight hours daily within the school building.

Every classroom and hallway will need hand sanitizers, disinfectant sprays, and additional protective gear and a higher level of sanitation daily. People coming into the building may have to have their temperature checked daily. When people are feeling under the weather, the option to go to work may be removed for them, and working from home could become an option to protect the safety of others.

Many of the things we required parents and visitors to come in to complete may be accepted electronically. The gathering for sports, physical education, bands, plays, and concerts will change drastically, if they happen at all. Parents may even be required to sign off regarding the school district liabilities, so their children can participate in activities that may be deemed a risk for exposure.

There is also the future of school districts' financial conditions. The possibility that the federal government will not provide the financial relief the state requires and if districts are losing 20 percent of the current school years' aid, this will cause significant problems for school business managers. It will force them into making decisions regarding several different dilemmas of program and personnel funding.

The financial impact will vary by district but could range from a couple hundred thousand to millions of dollars. The financial review and scrutiny for every purchase to prepare for the possibility of a loss in state aid means not having the revenue to support the school year's anticipated expenses.

Much goes on behind-the-scenes about the planning of doing more with less, layoffs, program changes, and using fund balance to cover the gap. School business officials have always enjoyed the challenges presented by these types of financial dilemmas, in the past, and most are confident that they have new experiences in their "management toolboxes" to deal with them more effectively and efficiently because of the recent journey through the turbulence of COVID-19.

The recommendation to anyone seated in a place of leadership, and especially those who oversee business/operations, is to know that the task is not to make the politically correct decision but to make the one that is best for the organization. The future is ever-changing, and with that change will require flexibility in developing plans for how everything will work in organizational sympatico.

In the educational world, school district business administrators will reflect throughout the day and even in their dreams about the following questions to be considered whenever a crisis occurs: How do we provide meals to our students daily, how do we clean and sanitize our buildings, how do we educate our students, and how do we finance and support the financial obligations of running a school district?

There may be many challenging days and many sleepless nights ahead. However, school business officials and now know from their recent experiences with COVID-19 that they will be able to cooperatively do it using the newly fine-tuned "flexible mindset" that enabled them to navigate the turbulence of this most recent punctuated equilibrium crisis. No one can predict the future, but what was once normal is not probably what will be the "new normal."

This "new normal" will have to be created by recognizing the value of continuously being flexible so that both individuals and organizations, like school districts, can adapt to the new future of educating students. The key to survival during and post any pandemic or crisis is flexibility and embracing change. When both of these are at the forefront and can be observed by those who follow the leader, it enables the leader to set the stage and truly empower a change mindset.

FUTURES FOR EDUCATION: POSSIBLE, PROBABLE, PREFERABLE

Possible Future of Education

The author of this chapter, herself an assistant superintendent for business and finance in the referenced case study school district, offers the following perspective for current and aspiring school business and financial officials:

Possible Future for Education

1. School cleaning will have to increase exponentially. Staff is pushing for either an increase in staff or an adjustment in staffing hours to cover what needs to occur more frequently.
2. Significant budgetary impacts occurred and will continue to occur due to the cost of personal protective equipment and having to purchase

masks, face shields, desk guards, cleaning supplies, gloves, and thermometers.
3. Food service will have to change drastically to allow all children to receive meals whether they are receiving learning virtually or in school. Students may be eating in classrooms or behind Plexiglass to allow for the proper safety precautions to be followed. The density on buses will have to decrease, and the regular school start and finish times adjusted to accommodate the different recommendations and guidelines provided to allow for an in-person teaching and learning environment.
4. Educational funding was threatened to be reduced. Between the last quarter's performance of sales and the funds utilized to assist with the pandemic, the state budget and sales tax revenue was estimated to drop drastically, which means less revenue received by school districts. As a result, we will be doing much more with far less.

Probable Future of Education

Some school districts were not able to allow students back during the 2020–2021 school year to degree that was initially predicted. With the rising numbers COVID-19 related cases and the requirements provided to school districts to ensure student and staff safety, it becomes increasingly difficult to follow the guidelines with no additional funding support. However, if students receive their learning entirely virtually, districts will be in a position where layoffs will have to occur to balance having to purchase technology to support students' virtual learning environment.

It is also probable that districts' funding will be cut by 20 percent, as previously expressed by the governor, accounting for millions of dollars that districts would not receive. I do believe that whatever the case is, food service will be required to function so all children can receive meals daily. Though this was the case at the end of the 2019–2020 school year, the continuation of this practice in the future becomes more difficult and costly to administer for an increased length of time.

Preferable Future of Education

It is generally recognized that administrators would prefer to open schools with 100 percent student return with in-school instruction in the 2021–2022 school year. As mentioned, many times throughout this book, it would be preferable if a plan was developed that fit the needs of students—allowing for their social and emotional needs to be addressed in a structured learning environment. As students return to a more normal type of schooling experience, there is a need to provide structure, physical activities, emotional support, social growth, and balanced nutritional food.

The pandemic has been brutal on all, especially the students whose academic, social, and emotional lives have changed tremendously. The steps that are taken now to address these changes will have lasting effects for years to come.

The preferable financial outcome would be that all school districts receive their total state aid funding expectations and additional federal funds to assist with the purchases to comply with personal protective equipment guidelines. It is the belief of this chapter author that all school systems cooperatively seek to purchase and implement the proper safety procedures so all children can come together and learn in a safe and structured learning environment.

FINAL THOUGHTS

It is incredible to look back over the last two years to provide insight from the lived experience. Some areas were spot on for what we anticipated coming forth, and there are others that we could not begin even to imagine. The 2020–2021 school year was not an easy one. Many school districts began in a 100 percent virtual model where all students remained at home or in a hybrid model with some process for dividing up the student population, so classrooms were at half capacity. This was expected along with some school shutdowns based upon the increases in infection rate.

These past school years, 2019–20; 2020–21; and 2021–22, were difficult years where everything you learned as a school leader was tested. Guidelines changed weekly in a way that made it impossible to keep up at times or provide reassurance to parents of what was forthcoming for their children. Plexiglass, barriers, and mask stuck around for more than one entire year and are continuing even as restrictions were lifted and schools were charged with doing more with less and the implementation of these changes were not free.

Business officials were charged with finding the funds, purchasing the equipment and supplies at whatever levels necessary to bring children back to school. Foodservice was constantly changing on the fly as schools went from a virtual or hybrid model to slowly bringing back 100 percent of the student population. There have never been so many bus runs created and alternate runs to accommodate the different learning models and the possibility of having to backtrack if the numbers continued to increase.

In summary, COVID-19 was something ubiquitously experienced, and many believed all districts would respond the same or employ the same type of approaches, but school district administrators across the country quickly learned that you have to do what works best for your local school district, your specific department, and your community. No two districts had the same plan, and many of the things implemented in one district did not or would not work in another, so allowing for stakeholder input and having transparent and appropriate communication provided for tremendous leadership success.

The world was far from black and white during the pandemic, and living in a world of grey is not easy when some form of structure is what people desired most during uncertain times, but the great leaders prevailed through the pandemic and gained new leadership characteristics through this lived experience.

If you can successfully lead through the pandemic, you can lead through anything because you gain an understanding of teamwork and effective communication and you have a more robust "administrative toolbox" than those who never experienced such a crisis!

KEY PRAGMATIC LEADERSHIP
TAKEAWAYS FROM CHAPTER 5

The following are key takeaways for school leaders to consider based on the crisis experiences of this assistant superintendent for business and finance:

- The leadership style for school leaders that seemed to be most effective throughout the pandemic was situational leadership. In situational leadership, the person leading must be flexible and modify their behavior to suit individuality rather than using one approach to lead the people, things, and ideas of the organization (Wall, 2019). This leadership style allowed for the necessary adaptable approach when the rules and guidelines swiftly changed from week to week and year to year.
- Situational leadership was instrumental in increasing collaboration between parents, students, staff, and the district leaders, which proved successful in getting through the 2020–21 school year together. It allowed the district leaders, building leaders, and students to adapt to different situations for succeeding years recognizing that the safety of all parties was a primary consideration.
- Situational leadership is supportive leadership, which is something everyone needed during a time of much uncertainty. The mental state of students and staff was challenged these past two years, and like a well-oiled machine, we kept pushing along to do all we could to provide the best educational opportunities for our children because of the leadership we received.
- In addition, many school district administrators, including the author of this chapter, learned through the "Lived Experiences" of leading school

systems through the COVID-19, that it was most prominent, "not to sweat the small stuff." Before the pandemic, when day-to-day operations were not progressing as expected, it could take up much administrative time fixing; now, after the pandemic, administrators are more flexible in such situations and possess a much more positive attitude toward finding solutions.

• A number of school district leaders, including this chapter author, realized how little individual control they really have, so working collectively to effectively solve problems associated with the people, things, and ideas of the school district that can be controlled is absolutely necessary.

• Finally, this author honestly believes that running a district requires a comprehensive team effort. Everyone's job is essential, and what they contribute to the organization is appreciated, because without each other, something is forgotten, not completed, or not considered, which could be detrimental to the team, especially when confronting an unexpected crisis.

REFERENCES

Hill, E. J., Grzywacz, J. G., Allen, S., Blanchard, V. L., Matz-Costa, C., Shulkin, S., & Pitt-Catsouphes, M. (2008). Defining and conceptualizing workplace flexibility. *Community, Work & Family, 11*(2), 149–163.

Walls, E. (2019). The value of situational leadership: The journal of the health visitor's association. *Community Practitioner, 92*(2), 31–33. Retrieved from https://ezproxy .niagara.edu/login?url=https://www-proquest-com.ezproxy.niagara.edu/scholarly -journals/value-situationalleadership/docview/2187546684/se-2?accountid=28213

Chapter 6

Human Resources During Crises

Emphasize the HUMAN in Human Resources

John E. McKenna and Moira H. Cooper

"When I was a boy and I would see scary things in the news, my Mother would say to me, look for the helpers. You will always find people who are helping. To this day especially in times of disaster, I remember my Mother's words and I am always comforted by realizing that there are still so many helpers, so many caring people in the world."

—Mr. Fred Rogers

This quote resonated with the authors of this chapter as they reflected on their leadership experiences as school district human resource administrators in dealing with the COVID-19 crisis. The authors had the distinct privilege to work with many amazing people who have gone above the call of duty to be helpers and make sure that the needs of students, staff, and families in this case study's large suburban school district were addressed to the greatest extent possible.

The members of the school district's support team who assisted the authors in the administration of the human resource department are truly the heroes who have put themselves at risk to help others. They provided motivation and inspiration to each other as well as to this chapter's authors whose belief in the genuine goodness of people was reconfirmed with a renewed confidence that the "high-touch" human approach to conducting school district operations will eventually result in the end to the current pandemic crisis and make school personnel and their leaders stronger and smarter to confront future crises that may unexpectantly occur.

It should be noted that one of the authors is the assistant superintendent for human resources in this case study school district and also served as acting superintendent during the pandemic crisis. The other author is an attorney who is employed as the school district's labor relations specialist. Both authors have extensive experience in human resource management.

IT WAS THE WORST OF TIMES THAT BROUGHT OUT THE BEST OF MOST PEOPLE

A crisis brings out the best in some people but it also brings out the worst in others. This pandemic has also revealed another kind of person. Those who like to criticize, condemn, and complain. The fault finders who like to cast stones, blame others, and magnify issues. People who use the crisis to attack the system because of unresolved past issues or philosophical differences. These are misguided people who say they are fighting for the students but they really have their own hidden agenda to hurt who they believe are their enemies.

The characteristics of helpers and complainers will be elaborated on later in this chapter. However, the human resource administration's perspective of dealing with the current crisis will be the initial topic reviewed. It is important to note that schools as well as other organizations are far from through this crisis ordeal and there are many more hurdles to clear and lessons to be learned in navigating through these unchartered turbulent waters.

This crisis journey has illustrated to school leaders that they must be willing to change quickly their typical modus operandi and recognize that what was right yesterday maybe be wrong today. The key to all decision making must be what school leaders believe it is in the best interest of the students. There are various perspectives on this and communication between all stakeholders is crucial in coming to the best decision. Safety is paramount!

Thorough analysis of data and research on the effects of students and their families must be seriously examined before future decisions can be made. School leaders must also consider the health and safety of the teachers, administrators, custodians, and secretaries who work closely with students on a daily basis. But an analysis of the history of this crisis in regards to the human resource department personnel and leadership in this case study suburban school district provides valuable insight that is useful for current and future school leaders. The following is a brief introduction to managing people, things, and ideas during the COVID-19 crisis experience from the Human Resource Administration perspective.

UNFORGETTABLE FRIDAY, MARCH 13, 2020

Like several other school districts across the country, Friday, March 13, 2020, was the last day for in-person school attendance for students in this school district for the 2019–2020 academic year. No one possessed the perception at that time COVID-19 global pandemic would impact school attendance for the rest of that year and the most of the following year.

On Monday March 16, 2020, Governor Andrew Cuomo issued an executive order closing all schools across New York. It was originally thought by school district leaders that this March closing would last a few weeks, and prepared accordingly. The prevailing perception was that people would self-quarantine, practice appropriate social distancing, and once the virus would be under control, school district teaching and learning as well as school operations would all be back to normal.

Unfortunately, that would not be the case. COVID-19 cases across New York sky-rocketed, and it became apparent rather quickly that this crisis was not going to end soon. Immediate plans needed to be made to ensure that students continued to learn and that district operations would function.

Other crucial areas that needed immediate attention included but were not limited to: feeding students who needed free and reduced lunches; providing appropriate technology to students; employee payroll and benefits; deep cleaning of facilities, budgeting, cost estimating for unexpected expenses such as personal protective equipment and materials; and deciding who were essential personnel during this crisis. So many decisions had to made so quickly, and no one had ever done anything like this before.

There were no strategic or tactical plans for operating within such a global pandemic and there was no time to prepare as change was thrust upon all education providers. School district leaders were forced to accept the challenge and "fight" it since there was no option to "flee" from it as leaders of a large educational organization in a community that values high quality education.

The following were some of the key actions of the administrators and their support personnel in the human resource department of this case study school district:

LABOR RELATIONS ISSUES

MOA's with Each Bargaining Unit

There were seven different bargaining units in this highly unionized school district representing both instructional and non-instructional personnel. These bargaining groups included school personnel such as: teachers, administrators, custodians, secretaries, computer support technicians, teacher aides, and food service helpers.

In addition, the school district also employs per diem non-union employees that includes many teaching substitutes and other temporary employees. Altogether, there were about four thousand employees of this school district in spring 2020. Each bargaining group has its own contract and is regulated with different guidelines and rules based on the Public Employees Relationship Board (PERB) of New York, which oversees employee rights.

As this strange crisis period began, school district administrators were expecting employees to perform their job functions from home to work, and thus, it was imperative that school leaders provided directives and guidelines for people to work from home. To help facilitate a smooth transition, the HR department developed Memorandums of Agreement (MOAs) with each bargaining unit.

These MOAs stated that employees were to work from home the best they could, but they must be working and available during their regular work hours, and that they could be called back into work at any time based on the discretion of the administration and the status of the pandemic crisis.

Shortcomings of the MOAs

The MOAs that were created were appropriate at the time they were developed because it was believed that there would be a "normal return" back to school in a few weeks. Subsequently, daily and weekly, the personnel administrators would await for additional information from the governor's office about the status of the pandemic. The official announcement that school would not resume for the remainder of the school year came on May 1, 2020. By that time, many issues had become apparent for dealing with this ubiquitous crisis.

For instance, the MOAs did not specifically identify the specific online platform teachers should utilize to communicate with students. This resulted in staff utilizing a variety of platforms including Zoom, Google Meet, Skype, and Webex to reach out to students. Some staff used traditional email, while others made personal phone calls.

There were no clear expectations for how to communicate. This was very confusing for the students and their parents. In addition, the MOAs did not specifically state the frequency and how often teachers and staff were to reach out to students. There was also confusion about assignments and grading practices.

The result was major inconsistencies in the delivery of instruction, frequency of teacher contact, online platforms being utilized, the amount of work assigned, the quality of the work assigned, and the grading practices utilized by the teachers. There were also questions about how to implement special areas such as art, music, gym, and library. Special services involving school counselors, social workers, psychologists, and academic intervention teachers needed to continue for students with expected legal fidelity.

There were also multiple special education issues that we needed to consider. Each special education student has an Individual Education Plan (IEP) that is mandated by the state and must be implemented. Some of these mandated services include speech therapy, occupational therapy, and physical therapy.

The initial MOAs between the school district and its various bargaining units lacked many specific details, as a result, additional issues continuously emerged as people worked through the crisis as best as they could without a detailed "game plan." Personnel administrators conducted several meetings with the principals and teachers to iron out all the problems that arose as the school district leaders identified how to deliver instruction and services to all students.

Solutions and Recommended Best Practices

Memorandums of Agreement need to be specific. They need to clearly identify what online platform all staff will utilize and how often they are expected to meet with students. They must also clearly communicate how many minutes a single session should be and how many sessions are expected to be taught each day. Directives must be clear and unambiguous. The ambiguity of the original MOA's caused confusion and resulted in disparity in the delivery of instruction.

Teachers who were progressive and proactive were quickly able to transition to an online format. They instinctively knew to reach out on a daily basis and set up online video conferences. They also knew how to post work for students and how to grade and provide feedback on assignments.

Proactive teachers also set up office hours online so students and parents could get individual feedback. Proactive teachers also did not hesitate to contact students and their parents directly to ensure students were actively participating or to simply check in to see how students were doing.

Unfortunately, not every teacher is a proactive, responsible professional. Multiple staff inappropriately interpreted the loose structure of the MOAs to mean that they did not have to do anything specific. They used the lack of specific language as an excuse to do as little as possible. In some cases, it was reported that some staff did nothing. Consequently, several parents complained to the principals, superintendent, and the Board of Education and demanded consistency.

The superintendent of schools put out a message to the instructional staff that they were to reach out to their students at least once a week using Zoom (or some form of video conferencing). The teachers' union responded that this was a change in working conditions, and the superintendent did not have the right to mandate this.

The superintendent clarified his remarks that it was not mandatory but it was best practice to reach out to students via some form of video conference on a regular basis. It was surprising to see the teachers' union push back on a common-sense suggestion that was obviously in the best interest of the students but not specifically addressed in the MOA.

The lesson was clear: The original MOAs needed to provide specific expectations for all staff in detail. The administration cannot assume that staff will act in the best interest of students. Unions will often act to protect their members and not do what is in the best interests of the students.

It was difficult for most residents of the school district to understand when unions protect staff that are not doing their jobs and fulfilling their responsibility to make sure that students get the best education possible. However, it was incumbent upon the administration to research and think out as many details as possible about any given situation before developing any future MOA.

It was also determined by the human resource administration to recommend that all MOAs created in response to a crisis situation specify a specific limited duration of time. In the case of COVID-19 the situation was unfolding so fast and changing from day to day, it was important to construct them in such a way that the administration can make appropriate modifications as necessary.

As a human resources administrator, it is imperative not to be stuck with a bad agreement that could be used against the district to protect inappropriate practice and against doing what is in the best interests of the students.

Payroll Challenges

During the COVID-19 crisis, it was imperative that all district payroll functions remained operational. The administration made the decision that all employees would remain on the payroll and receive paychecks for the remainder of the 2020–2021 school year, regardless if they came to work or not.

This included all employees from all seven bargaining units. At the beginning of the crisis, no one was not sure how long normal school operations would be curtailed and it was anticipated that schools would be back in session before the end of the school year. Even after it became apparent that the 2019–2020 school year would be abruptly concluded, this school district, like so many others, guaranteed that all employees on the payroll to would receive their regular negotiated compensation and benefits.

To ensure that payroll would continue to function normally, arrangements had to be made with the IT department to set up the proper technology so payroll staff could perform a portion of their work from home. However, given the confidentially requirements associated with processing payroll, many aspects could not be done from home.

Therefore, the payroll department had to develop a regular schedule for some key employees to come into their traditional school district work spaces to process the payroll so people could be paid on time.

This was a pragmatic necessity because most employees have direct deposit and pay their monthly bills automatically based on their biweekly check. If the checks were not completed and deposited on time it could be financially disastrous for employees. Furthermore, people need to eat and pay for the necessities to live and support their families. Payroll is truly essential and must not stop, not even for a week, no matter the crisis.

Challenges With Employee Benefits

During the pandemic, it was imperative that employees had access to all of their medical benefits. Like so many other school districts, this large suburban school district has multiple employees who have serious health issues and it was imperative for the administration to ensure their access to the care and medications they needed. There is also important paperwork that needs to be completed in a timely fashion to ensure that certain staff receive essential medical services.

Some employees contracted COVID-19 and needed medical attention. Some were seriously ill and required a ventilator. In addition, there were many employees who gave birth during the crisis and others who needed emergency procedures such heart surgery. Also, there were some staff who required emergency dental procedures as well.

Normal health issues did not stop during this crisis, and people needed their medical benefits and information to be current to receive treatments. Unfortunately, some doctors, medical facilities, and organizations required quick verification to allow treatments to occur, which heightened the stress upon the human resource department personnel.

Therefore, the benefits personnel could not take a day off. But, like other similar school districts, it is also important to clarify that the "benefits department" consists of one person. With the assistance of the IT department, it was possible to allow her to perform some tasks from home, but given the nature of the work and the confidentiality issues that are associated with this department, many of the other tasks needed to be completed on-site.

There is also daily mail that contains crucial medical information with time sensitive information. This crisis made it very clear that we need to cross train other employees to help support this area in times of turmoil.

MAJOR HUMAN RESOURCES TOPICS
DURING CRISIS MANAGEMENT

The following represents a brief summary of some of the major issues and challenges faced by administrators in the human resources department of this case study's school district during the COVID-19 pandemic. A bulleted format is used in order to present the material in a concise manner. Each area presented encompasses many specific details and nuances that cannot be fully addressed within the scope of this publication.

However, this is meant to be a summary and overview of the major challenges faced, the lessons learned up to this time, and recommendations for the future. But, it is definitely realized by the administrators of the human resources division of this school district that this issue is ever-changing, and updates are constantly needed as school leaders navigate through these unprecedented times.

Staffing

As the 2020–2021 school year approached, the pandemic was still raging across the country and causing serious problems and safety concerns for school districts. The pandemic and the safety requirements for social distancing had major implications on school districts. Furthermore, many states required that school districts offer a remote-learning option to families who did not feel safe sending their children to school.

This became a major challenge for school districts across the country, as it was necessary for school leaders to determine how to deliver remote instruction effectively and efficiently while maintaining high academic standards and staying within their budget parameters.

It was imperative to research possible models and make specific plans well in advance before implementing any changes to instructional models or staffing configurations. Most districts were given the choice to implement a fully remote model where all students learned from home or a hybrid model where some children learn from home while others learned in school settings. It was up to each district to determine which model worked best for their community.

The following are some recommendations that all school districts should consider when determining a learning model that is right for them in preparing for crisis management:

- Proactively start researching best practice as soon as possible.
- Develop a clear vision, mission, and goals in case of a punctuated change in operations.
- Establish committees of stakeholders to work collaboratively as a team
- Multiple committees should be formed to work on: the instructional model, the social–emotional well-being of students, the creative engagement of all students (both remote and hybrid), the future of the instructional model, and implications moving forward.
- Develop a clear plan with specific action steps to phase in the model. Be concise and clear.
- Set up a schedule of meetings and monitor the progress moving forward (Note: it will be necessary to conduct several meetings to successfully develop a learning model. Be prepared to meet every day/all day for several weeks).
- Develop appropriate/ongoing staff develop support system to support staff, listen to their concerns, monitor progress, and make proper adjustments.
- Analyze the technology needs of the personnel and develop a technology plan that ensures students and staff have the proper technology to successfully implement the program. Make frequent tests to ensure technology is working appropriately.

Unemployment Claims and Issues

Challenges:

- One of the greatest challenges in benefits administration was handling the increase in unemployment claims and the volume of fraudulent unemployment claims that were filed in employees' names. School districts establish annual budgets for unemployment benefits based on foreseeable projections. However, during this crisis year, the pandemic event more than quadrupled the costs for many employers.
- Moreover, unemployment expenses were further inflated by numerous fraudulent or ineligible claims that the school districts ultimately have to protest. This forced school district leaders to reallocate funds or utilize reserve funds to offset the increased costs.

  School administrators also had to reevaluate future budget decisions based on the likely possibility that the COVID-19 crisis will continue into the next school year. This also resulted in potential staff layoffs, budget cuts in other areas, and reductions in facilities, equipment, and capital project expenditures. The pandemic crisis has forced all districts to examine their budgets and prepare for necessary cuts and adjustments going forward into the next school year.

- The COVID-19 CARES Act requires the federal government to reimburse employers for approximately half of the cost of the newly increased unemployment benefits since March of 2020. It is still unclear how and when that will happen.

   The CARES Act not only increased the unemployment benefit amount per employee, but also extended the time frame during which employees are eligible to collect benefits. The time frame for benefits may also continue longer than usual (i.e., during the summer) because school leaders cannot yet determine whether employees can have reasonable assurance of employment for next school year.

- While working remotely, it is very difficult for school district employees to monitor unemployment claims since related correspondence are mailed to the districts' physical addresses.

- The New York State Unemployment Office was overwhelmed with the increased number of filings, causing further delay and confusion. For example, NYS has not yet responded to any of the local school districts' protests and challenges to ineligible claims. This results in benefits being paid out to some employees who are not actually eligible for benefits.

Solutions and Recommended Best Practices

- The human resources department had to develop a system using laptops at home and home scanners to process cases and stay on top of required operations remotely. The human resources administration and staff had to use numerous resources to facilitate remote work but still had to come in at least weekly to continue getting mail and to issue and mail paychecks to staff.

- There must be improved and direct communication with the New York State Department of Labor and other relevant law enforcement agencies to flag fraudulent unemployment claims since the process dealing with fraudulent claims must be on a case-by-case basis.

- Human resources administrators communicated with union leadership and provided general information and directions to be given to affected staff members. Communications directly to affected staff members were also necessary in order to provide contact information for the NYS DOL and law enforcement agencies such as the FBI. However, the human resources department needed to monitor those communications with union leadership and affected employees to decide the appropriate scope of communications.

- In addition, the human resources department personnel did not want to alarm all staff members by sending out mass emails that did not apply to everyone. Instead, they wanted employees who were actually impacted or likely to be impacted to be informed of the facts.
- Also, communication is more difficult in such a widespread crisis situation because employees were all basically working from home and not checking their email on a regular basis. This illustrated that perhaps a broader and more specific communication system would be more effective in retrospect for future cases.

Employee Benefits

Challenges

- School district personnel had to monitor and review mail from the U.S. Postal Service and do physical check-ins on-site on a regular basis. Employees from different departments were required to coordinate schedules and communications.
- Regular communications to staff were required, such as when there were changes to the school districts' health insurance plans and benefits. For example, many districts opted in to telehealth opportunities during school shutdowns to expand accessibility for staff members in quarantine.

  Staff had to be made aware of the new remote healthcare options. This was sometimes difficult for staff members who were not monitoring email regularly while at home. School leaders were not prepared for these issues, and were reactive in communications and providing information regarding remote medical options as opposed to being proactive.
- Teledoc and telemedicine remote health care options had very low utilization prior to COVID-19, and experienced a significant increase in utilization during the pandemic. These systems require access to phone and/or video technology in order to connect with health care providers. Employers who newly added teledoc or telemedicine during the onset of the pandemic were forced to set up utilization protocol and cost structures in response to the increased demand for these services.
- The COVID-19 pandemic was considered a "qualifying event" for health care elections, increasing the need for streamlined communication with employees regarding eligibility to opt in or out of insurance plans, flexible spending accounts, and premium deductions.

Solutions and Recommended Best Practices

- School district leaders must provide school employees with the technology to quickly adapt to working from home and provide access to virtual private network connections (VPNs). This includes laptops, scanners, printers, and so on. VPN capabilities allow access to specialized software and protected documents that are saved to work hard drives from home. Working proactively with IT staff ahead of time and developing both strategic plans and tactical options would provide a faster and easier transition when a crisis occurs.
- Develop a system for mail delivery and receipt, including the designation of personnel for specific roles. Collaborate with facilities staff and the U.S. Postal Service to ensure regular mail delivery at a centralized location, and then distribute the mail via a designated courier. Human resources staff may assist by applying postage and sorting the mail to ensure proper delivery to the appropriate parties.
- Use email and regular mail to communicate with all employees regarding access to remote health supports such as Teledoc or telemedicine and other health insurance plan changes. Emails should include links and informational attachments. School district administrators should also maintain regular communication with union leadership in advance to ensure that all staff receives information and understands how to access benefits and health services. Coordination with union leadership ensures a united and consistent message.

Finding Daily Substitutes for Staff

Challenges

During widespread crisis like the COVID-19 pandemic, it was extremely difficult to find substitutes for all staff from all bargaining units. People felt it was too risky and was not worth the money to come in and substitute for a daily wage. Many were collecting stimulus money from the federal government and were getting more money on unemployment than they would working so it was very challenging to get people to agree to come in and substitute. This was an issue for all areas including teachers, custodians, cleaners, bus drivers, secretaries, aides, and assistants.

There were multiple classrooms in this district that needed substitutes daily. This caused major dilemmas in schools and it was necessary to find solutions quickly because students needed to be taught daily by a qualified teacher and parents would only be patient for so long. They wanted and deserved the best possible highest quality experiences for their children. It was also a major challenge to find substitute cleaners and custodians.

The pandemic caused the administrators to have major increases in building cleaning responsibilities and expenses. Each day there were areas that needed constant cleaning and disinfecting. It was necessary to hire additional cleaning staff but it was not easy to find people willing to take these jobs at this time.

In addition, the school district administration experienced this same problem in terms of other school support service personnel such as bus drivers and cafeteria staff. It was a major dilemma and the district administration was forced to think outside the box and come up with creative solutions to solve such daily problems.

Solutions and Recommended Best Practices

One major solution to this school district's teacher shortage problem was the utilization of building-based substitutes. A building-based substitute is a certified teacher who is assigned full-time to a specific building for the duration of the year. It was discovered that if substitute teachers were promised a specific location for a guaranteed significant amount time, they were willing to commit to the position.

This was a win-win situation, as the district was able to secure substitutes that were necessary to cover classes and they were given steady employment and the possibility of future employment if they do a great job.

Principals in this school district were told that they could each have five regular substitute teachers in their buildings each day for the school year. If a building did not need them on any given day they could share them with other schools. This worked extremely well as the district administration was able to successfully cover classes on a regular basis.

Regarding cleaning staff and cafeteria workers, the district administrative got very creative and let the cleaning staff help out in the cafeterias and other cafeteria staff help with the cleaning duties whenever possible. This was another win-win situation because it allowed the administration to cover multiple areas with the same staff and let the workers pick up extra hours and in some cases overtime. This "staff sharing" model was very effective and will be employed in the future even after the current pandemic crisis is over.

The most challenging situation confronting this school district and others across the country was trying to find bus drivers and substitutes for the drivers. The school administration posted positions multiple times but could not get people to apply. It was noticed that many parents were driving their children to school to avoid close contact with others, and this freed up seats on our busses.

The parents of children attending schools in this district were surveyed and asked if some would be willing to commit to driving their children full-time. Many agreed that they would do this, and this allowed the administration to consolidate busses and bus run routes. The result of this decision was that most of the students of this school district were successfully transported to schools and social distancing guidelines set by the state of New York were followed.

Thus, finding substitutes during a crisis to fill in for regular staff on a day-to-day basis was not easy but with creativity, ingenuity, and persistence this district, like so many others, was able to adequately staff all areas and get through the 2020–21 school year successfully.

Leaves of Absence and the FFCRA, ADA, and FMLA

Challenges

Along with daily absences it was necessary for the school human resources administration to address long and short-term leaves of absence provided by federal and state legislation as well as contractual provisions that allowed staff to take extended leaves. The most challenging situation regarding leaves was implementing the Families First Coronavirus Response Act (FFCRA, 2020). This federal legislation required that employers provide paid sick leave and expanded family and medical leave to employees who qualified.

Under the FFCRA, an employee qualifies for expanded family leave if the employee is caring for a child whose school or place of care is closed (or child care provider is unavailable) for reasons related to COVID-19. All employees of covered employers are eligible for two weeks of paid sick time for specified reasons related to COVID-19. Employees employed for at least thirty days are eligible for up to an additional ten weeks of paid family leave to care for a child under certain circumstances related to COVID-19.

Under the FFCRA, an employee qualifies for expanded family leave if the employee is caring for a child whose school or place of care is closed (or child care provider is unavailable) for reasons related to COVID-19. According to the U.S. Department of Labor, under the FFCRA, an employee qualifies for paid sick time if the employee is unable to work (or unable to telework) due to a need for leave because the employee:

1. Is subject to a Federal, State, or local quarantine or isolation order related to COVID-19;
2. Has been advised by a health care provider to self-quarantine related to COVID-19;

3. Hs experiencing COVID-19 symptoms and is seeking a medical diagnosis;
4. Is caring for an individual subject to an order described in (1) or self-quarantine as described in (2);
5. Is caring for a child whose school or place of care is closed (or child care provider is unavailable) for reasons related to COVID-19; or
6. Is experiencing any other substantially-similar condition specified by the Secretary of Health and Human Services, in consultation with the Secretaries of Labor and Treasury.

Given the above parameters, it is clear to see how this legislation prompted many employees to put in for leaves of absence under the FFCRA. In addition, multiple staff applied for traditional leaves provided by the Family and Medical Leave Act (FMLA) or for accommodations pursuant to the American with Disabilities Act (ADA).

The FMLA provides eligible employees up to twelve weeks of unpaid leave per year and requires group health benefits to be maintained during the leave as if employees continued to work instead of taking leave. Employees are also entitled to return to their same or an equivalent job at the end of their FMLA leave (U.S. Department of Labor, Family and Medical Leave Act, 1993).

The ADA requires employers to provide reasonable accommodations to qualified applicants or employees. A "reasonable accommodation" is a change that accommodates employees with disabilities so they can do the job without causing the employer "undue hardship." The ADA also requires public entities to make their programs, services, and activities accessible to individuals with disabilities (US Department of Justice, Civil Rights Division, Americans with Disabilities Act, 1990).

Consequently, the requirements of the FMLA, FFCRA, and ADA presented many challenges to school district human resource administrators during this crisis situation. They and their support personnel had to rethink how to implement leaves and accommodate employee working requests.

Solutions and Recommended Best Practices

Given the challenges presented by the pandemic and the parameters from the various opportunities for leaves of absence, there were some very important lessons learned in dealing with this unique situation and perhaps other future similar crises.

First, it was recognized that all school leaders and their support personnel needed to be flexible and understanding. This was truly an extraordinary time and the human resource office leaders and support staff could not adhere to rigid policies and practices that did not meet the needs of this crisis situation. Human resource personnel listened carefully to each individual concern, developed new forms for school employees to fill out where they could describe their unique situation, and did everything in their power to accommodate requests as much as possible.

The human resource office team worked with the unions and made agreements that this was a special year and that many of the solutions implemented during this crisis would be done on a non-precedented basis. MOAs would need to include a "sunset clause" to guarantee non-continuance without additional negotiated agreement.

Most importantly, the school district human resource administrators and their support team learned that many people could work effectively and efficiently from home. Teachers, at all levels of the instructional spectrum, could teach remotely, school office secretaries could perform most of their duties from home, and many administrative functions could also be done from home.

But, cleaners, custodians, lunchroom workers, and bus drivers had to report daily since their services were essential "student custodial services" directly needed to effectively continue learning. But the administration tried to be as flexible as possible with their work schedules and continued to recognize their contributions to the successful operations of schools during a crisis.

Working remotely was truly game-changing, and the Hyflex instructional model that was implemented in this school district where students in the classroom and at home learn together using webcams and document cameras was revolutionary and will probably change the delivery of instruction forever.

CONDUCTING INTERVIEWS AND HIRING PROCEDURES

Challenges

Since many professional staff members were taking leaves of absence there was a need to hire teachers for a variety of subjects and levels. The district administration also offered multiple instructional models that required different staffing needs. At the high school and middle school levels, a Hyflex model of concurrent instruction that simultaneously taught students in school and at home at the same time was offered to all students.

At the elementary level, one of the models offered was a hybrid model in which students were divided into two cohorts whereby, on alternating days, one group would come to school and receive in-person instruction, while the other group would stay home and work on teacher-made asynchronous work.

The groups would rotate so that only half of the students would be in school on any given day. This allowed for proper social distancing to occur in classrooms. The elementary level also offered a fully remote model in which students stayed at home and were taught by a designated remote teacher.

Providing these various models created the need to hire additional professional staff to ensure that all models could be implemented successfully. New solutions were necessary to help meet these identified teaching-learning needs during such a crisis.

Solutions and Recommended Best Practices

It was necessary to hire multiple staff to make the various instructional models of this district work but hiring committees could not be rapidly formed because of social distancing requirements. Therefore, the human resource department quickly transformed the hiring process to a remote model.

All of the interview trainings and question development sessions were conducted remotely and then all of the interviews were conducted remotely as well. New training guidelines that emphasized confidentiality were developed, and there was no video or audio taping and sharing of this information over social media.

Overall, the new method of remote interviews worked very well. It allowed the human resources team to interview many candidates including people who lived in other geographic areas. The process took longer than conventional interviews but was very effective.

There were also some technology problems that hindered the process sometimes but participants in the process learned to tell candidates at the beginning of the process to be prepared, log in fifteen minutes ahead of time and check their equipment, have headphones and, if disconnected, to log back in as quickly as possible. Interviewees were also asked them to have a phone available as an audio backup for the interview. Remote interviews worked so well that the school district administration is definitely planning to utilize them into the future even after the pandemic is over.

PROBABLE, POSSIBLE, AND PREFERABLE
FUTURES FOR CRISIS MANAGEMENT

Possible Future

Most likely, school district leaders will continue to do the best they can with the conditions they are presented with related to crisis management. Based on the experiences of the COVID-19 crisis, school districts leaders will work with authorities from their state and local health departments and continue to monitor the pandemic testing data daily to check for trends in positivity rates, contact trace all positive cases, appropriately quarantine all people exposed to viruses and ensure our schools follow all the safety protocols and procedures to maximize the safety of students and staff.

School district human resource administrators will continue to work with the district employees regarding their respective leaves of absence and instances of quarantine and find ways to utilize long term and per diem substitutes to cover classes effectively. In summary, district leaders will continue to be reactive to the conditions they are faced with and meet the challenges the best they can as problems arise.

Probable Future

Given the challenges that school districts experienced through this pandemic crisis, their respective leadership hopefully will be better prepared to meet the future challenges presented by COVID-19 or any other unexpected natural or man-made crises. All school districts should have written safety plans that include: social distancing requirements, mask wearing protocols, PPE requirements, and specific procedures for lunch rooms and busses.

They should also have clear protocols for cleaning and sanitizing buildings as well as hand washing stations and the ability to perform temperature checks daily on students and staff. As the vaccine for COVID-19 is rolling out school districts will be able to phase students back into school. Hopefully all students will be able to return to full in person instruction.

Districts most probably will have learned from the past and will have proactive plans in place to maximize safety for students and staff. School leaders district must also be prepared to implement remote instruction and have asynchronous work ready if the probability arises that schools need to be quarantined due to a resurgence of the pandemic at any time.

Preferable Future

In the preferable future, the pandemic crisis will be under control and school leaders will be able to bring all students back to school settings full time. School districts will have the capability to transition to remote learning at any time, offering high quality remote instruction. In this scenario, every student has their own electronic device and every classroom has multiple cameras and a big screen to allow students to learn in school and at home simultaneously.

There will be multiple teachers to support the students in classroom settings both in person and remotely. Having remote teachers and teaching assistants available will be essential to support online learners. School district human resources administrators will also secure a team of building-based substitute teachers for each school of the district to ensure that students always have a highly qualified teacher to support them remotely and in person. These substitutes will participate in professional development and be familiar with the daily operations of the school so they will be able to support the school in many capacities.

School district leaders in the preferable future will also develop a catalog of online asynchronous courses that can be offered at any time throughout the year. These courses will provide interactive, meaningful activities that students will be able to complete at their own pace. School districts must also work with colleges and universities to develop online courses that count for college credit. This will allow high school students to earn college credit and prepare them to be college and career ready.

FINAL THOUGHTS

Throughout the early stages of the 2020 global pandemic, the authors of this chapter and their human resource colleagues specifically learned many valuable lessons about providing organizational support for people. First, it was learned that it is imperative to be flexible in times of crisis. During a crisis, while legislation, rules, and regulations continued to evolve, it was crucial to continue to monitor and adapt internal school district policies to the ever-changing landscape.

Secondly, it was also crucial to listen to all stakeholders and gain valuable insight from relevant questions and feedback, and remain situationally aware, in order to make the best decisions possible. The human resource personnel, both individually as well as their office staff collectively, needed to be acute listeners to ensure that the best possible decisions were made to meet the unique crisis exacerbated needs of district employees.

The individual circumstances and exceptional situations that arise during a crisis must be addressed in a very personal "high-touch" style. It is incumbent on human resource leaders to keep the "Human" in their interactions and the interactions of their staff with everyone they encounter. They need to model the genuine caring for others that they expect of others.

Thirdly, every situation that came to the attention of the human resource personnel was different, and there could not be a "one size fits all" solution to each and every problem. Effective human resource leaders and their support staff evaluated each situation with an open mind and implemented creative solutions as necessary. Effective leaders also utilized foresight to protect employer rights to adapt to future situations based on their knowledge of the current realities.

Finally, proactive leaders understood that cultivating and maintaining positive relationships were key factors in successfully navigating the crisis throughout all of its stages during its two-year history. Relationships were the foundation for building trust and enabling positive lines of communication. When positive relationships were formed by leaders, then their organizations were able to overcome obstacles and became exponentially stronger as a team with many united interests and goals.

Subsequently, educational leaders must always strive to ensure that all stakeholders are made aware of information and updates in real time. The proactive leader establishes a communication system which prepares individuals to pivot quickly in times of crisis. This includes addressing anticipated questions and concerns, and utilizing different modes of communication (e.g., email, text messaging, voice messages, social media, and websites) to make certain that messaging is as inclusive and accessible as possible.

KEY PRAGMATIC LEADERSHIP
TAKEAWAYS FROM CHAPTER 6

- *Communicate, Communicate, Communicate!:* Leaders must constantly communicate their plans and expectations clearly and concisely. During a crisis a conscientious leader will intentionally over communicate to proactively ensure all stakeholders know and understand what is always happening.
- *Flexibility and adaptability are essential*: Crisis situations are fluid and changing constantly. An effective leader needs to constantly monitor conditions and gain awareness of the situation. A proactive leader must have an open mindset and be willing to adapt plans immediately to meet the needs of an ever-changing environment.
- *Cultivate relationships and build a team*: An effectual leader knows that he/she cannot do it alone. To be successful, a leader must forge positive relationships and mobilize others to get actively involved in the problem-solving process. It is also imperative to engage others and tap into their skills and talents. This is how new ideas are generated and a preferable future is realized.
- *Provide time and resources to complete the mission*: A leader cannot expect the staff to be successful if they are not provided the proper equipment and training to implement the task. Efficient leaders make sure that they strategically plan to ensure that they have the proper materials and develop a realistic timeline that allows for learning and support.
- *Be positive and provide affirmation*: Successful leaders understand that their staff need positive feedback and reinforcement. They recognize

the importance of optimism and make sure they celebrate successes and acknowledge the efforts of their staff even when they fall short of a goal. Effective leaders in a crisis embrace the power of empathy and outwardly show their staff patience, kindness, and gratitude.

REFERENCES

US Department of Labor, Families First Coronavirus Response Act, Employer Paid Leave Requirements, 2020.

US Department of Labor, Family and Medical Leave Act, 1993.

United States Department of Justice, Civil Rights Division, Americans With Disabilities Act, 1990.

Chapter 7

Commencing New Leadership Positions During Crises

Finding an Appropriate Leadership Conceptual Framework to Address Unexpected Personal and Professional Challenges

Michelle Grimes

BACKGROUND INFORMATION

This chapter is based on leadership positions to which the author was appointed during the global pandemic which provided her with unique perpectives of managing people, things, and ideas as a relatively new leader in two different educational organizations. The author is a senior administrator who has served as a faculty member and leaders in the Ontario college system for over fifteen years. She has dedicated the better part of her career to polytechnic education.

When the pandemic was first declared in March 2020, she had just started a dean's role at new institution a mere seven weeks before campuses closed at colleges in Ontario, Canada. She was dropped into a new leadership paradigm that abruptly pivoted with little warning or time to prepare. Subsequently, she left that role in October 2020 to move back to her previous college and soon after assumed the dean's role at that institution.

Postsecondary institutional leaders in Ontario, Canada, like others throughout the world, have faced many hurdles, but none parallel the immense challenges that faced higher education administrators in the midst of the

COVID-19 pandemic. The move to online learning, enrollment declines, and financial pressures, in addition to health and safety concerns of COVID-19, created a VUCA environment: volatile, uncertain, complex, and ambiguous.

THE REALITIES OF VUCA IN CRISIS CONTEXT

The COVID-19 pandemic is poised to be one of the most impactful change events in the history of modern postsecondary education. In March 2020, widespread physical distancing closed colleges and university campuses, pushing most higher education programming toward remote and online learning (Jeffords, 2020).

Travel restrictions and environmental uncertainty led to enrolment and budgetary pressures, as the sector faced an uncertain economic future. Colleges and universities could not rely on norms, processes, routines, and schedules that form so much of institutional life in higher education. COVID-19 punctuated the equilibrium of almost all aspects of society, and higher education was no different.

In Ontario, this paradigm played out at community colleges, where applied, in-person experiential learning is a guiding principle of the system (Dennison & Gallagher, 2011). While online and remote learning has increased in recent years, the majority of programs in the Ontario college system were still being delivered in person. In March 2020, administrators, faculty, and staff began to move learning and support services to a virtual environment to enable the semester to continue without much ease or enthusiasm.

As a result, college employees had to rapidly upskill their digital acumen to be able to achieve this imperative. Likewise, students had to reframe their expectations of postsecondary education and their own ways of learning. Meanwhile, Ontario colleges faced an additional pressure: International enrollment was likely to decline for the next year or more.

After a decade of reliance upon international enrolment to make up for comparatively low levels of government grant funding (Basen, 2019), financial pressures were predicted, as colleges grappled with significant budgetary shortfalls, just as the province introduced a performance-based funding model (Usher, 2019). "So many variables to deal with in so little time," was a mantra of most Ontraio higher education leaders as their personal and professional frustration and stress levels increased dramatically.

This global pandemic phenomenon represented a major crisis for colleges, requiring them to rethink all aspects of their strategies and operations. Crises, typically, have a *response* phase followed by a *recovery* phase (Zdziarski, Dunkel, & Rollo, 2007). Although Ontario colleges are currently still in the *response* phase in 2021, at the time of writing they are poised to enter a *recovery* phase, eventually. Colleges will no doubt emerge changed due to this period of rapid organizational learning and societal upheaval.

Organizational learning occurs when conditions are such that most actors in the scenario feel a sense of psychological safety, are able to experiment, and have faith in the organization's leaders (Higgins et al., 2012). Those that learn quickly during a crisis are better positioned to recover and grow after it has passed (Drennan, McConnell & Stark, 2014). However, when faced with crisis, leadership tends to emerge in informal ways (Moerschell & Lao, 2012), a phenomenon that is often only obvious in hindsight (Veil, 2011) as this author has observed at two different organizations.

Punctuated equilibrium theory (Baumgartner, Jones & Mortenson, 2014) serves as a key theoretical model to help explain the pandemic disruption and resulting changes within organizations, as well as the potential for future organizational change (Romanelli & Tushman, 1994).

In higher education, there are few studies related to punctuated equilibrium and postsecondary education, and none involving Ontario colleges. Therefore, there was no strategic plan book or resource list for higher education leaders to reference as they contemplated managing the people, things, and ideas under their specific role purview during this crisis.

The pandemic disruption represents the biggest crisis the Ontario college system has ever faced—but also a tremendous opportunity to reimagine education for the twenty-first century. However, colleges need to be ready with reliable references to assist leaders in reframing norms and expectations to allow for innovation in academic delivery and support services.

Educational leaders were tested, and often frustrated, countless times throughout the initial stages of the global pandemic as it was necessary to navigate through myriad problems in an ever-changing environment. Change management in a time of crisis is a challenging undertaking, as leaders needed to manage the changes required to survive and thrive as an organization (Marshall et al., 2021). Communication, compassion, and collaboration are attributes sought by followers during times of crisis (Eagly et al., 2020; Gartzia et al., 2012).

For colleges, these included: meeting the needs of students, staff, and faculty and to continue to move the organization forward in terms of the vision and mission. In addition, the nurturing role that leaders were expected to play for their followers was exacerbated as there were increased physical and emotional impacts on team members as the crisis wore on, and personal and professional stress levels increased exponentially.

So many of the problems that college institutions in Canada faced included aspects that stemmed beyond adjusting systems and structures and were mainly due to adding instructional complexity to the context.

For example, faculty could theoretically teach online from home—but some did not have adequate technology; some had young children or elderly parents to care for; some had low levels of comfort with online learning; a few had sick family members, or were sick themselves; and still others had mental health issues that rose to the surface due to the confinement period. There were multiple problems, many without any previously verified solutions that leaders need to address spontaneously as crisis time seemd to move much more quickly than regular time.

Education is definitely a people business as evidenced by the fact that most school budgets are heavily oriented to providing for human services like teaching, administration, and organizational support including student services, facility cleaning, security, and cafeteria.

High-touch interventions, in which change is facilitated through personal connections, are more effective in promoting change efforts in educational environments as they can more easily address context specific to an institution, or sub-units within an institution (Polka, 2007).

EFFECTIVE CHANGE ZONE MODEL

Most traditional change management models tend to prescribe a systematic process that is carefully planned, implemented, evaluated, and recycled. Such a mode wasl not appropriate for reference during the chaotic management days associated with this global pandemic. Generally, those models did not lend themselves to this VUCA (volatile, uncertain, complex, and ambiguous)-oriented crisis environment.

However, the *Effective Change Zone* (ECZ) model articulated by Polka (2007), based on a synthesis of key well researched and reliable socio-psychology concepts, considers the *organizational, professional,* and *personal* needs of an organization and its members as a way to effectively manage change.

This model allows for flexibility, overlap, and movement between those three areas of needs: organizational, professional, and personal in any organization and was useful to apply in human service contexts such as higher education, especially in times of crises. This high-touch approach promotes trust-building within the team, which then sets the stage for authentic organizational change and learning.

In the early weeks and months of the pandemic, many college administrators, including the author of this chapter, spent countless sleepless nights considering the organizational, professional, and personal needs within their respective educational organization.

Unfortunately, for the author and others like her in relatively new positions in different organizations, they were still learning about their new institutions and teams, while also learning to steer those teams through a crisis without a solid understanding of the people, the organization, and the culture.

For many administrators in such a relatively new professional context, each decision felt urgent, but carried weighty consequences; meanwhile, implementation had to be swift, but flexible, to adapt to changing conditions. Even seemingly simple solutions had layers of complexity, creating additional problems to be solved.

Computer-mediated communications impeded a high-touch approach at a time when teams needed more interaction with leaders than ever. For these newer administrators finding their way to the ECZ (Polka, 2007), was, and still remains, a significant challenge.

Rapid Change and Resilience

The decision of many Ontario colleges to move most of their programs online for the fall semester in 2020 seems inevitable in hindsight. In late April 2020, however, many college administrators struggled with the decision, as uncertainty took hold. Most of those educational leaders had already moved the remainder of the winter semester online, and students and faculty alike were seeking answers about their courses.

Administrative leadership teams at several colleges held many sessions using Zoom, a video conferencing software, to debate the options. The following were key questions that could be heard during administrative leadership team meetings at institutions worldwide: What if the virus fades? What if it lasts for months? What if they find a cure? What if they don't? What if we stay closed and other institutions open up? What if we open and everyone else stays closed?

Obviously, there was the perception that some programs could easily move to remote delivery, whereas, other programs with accreditation or applied skill requirements, needed face-to-face delivery. Some leaders were reluctant to commit to a firm decision with so little certainty and so much at stake. While others, by contrast, wanted to move forward, whatever the decision.

Some higher education leaders seemed ready to accept the opportunities presented by this crisis to significantly change the structure and format of higher education systems in Ontario, but other leaders were determined to maintain a "normalcy status" as much as they could. However, to add to the management chaos at each institutional site, there were leaders all long that spectrum. This made genuine consensus buiding very difficult at a time when decisions needed to be made very quickly.

As a compromise, deans at some colleges were tasked with completing scenario-planning in their schools based on several possibilities:

1. As-normal, face-to-face delivery
2. Online delivery for the early part of the semester, followed by a return to campus
3. Most programs online, with some programs offering limited, face-to-face delivery in some courses
4. Fully online delivery

The planning process helped determine the feasibility of each scenario for each program. The work allowed senior leaders to gain a bird's-eye view of which scenario worked best across program areas, while also laying some groundwork for other scenarios, should conditions change. In the author's case, her institution ultimately moved forward with the third scenario, but the process helped facilitate organizational change by meeting the organization's needs consistent wwith the research of Polka (2007).

Cooperative Component of ECZ Planning

A key aspect of organizational planning since for the past sixty years has been stressed that planning for change should be a *cooperative* venture, one that includes a large group of stakeholders, in order for change to be both innovative and sustainable because there would be numerous supporters of it.

The scenario planning process in one of the case study higher education instutions in Ontario involved faculty teams and associate deans, who are closest to the operational requirements of each program. In many cases, those teams consulted other employees, such as technologists, support staff and curriculum consultants, to solicit input for the plans.

The plans were then reviewed by senior leaders before submission. This process provided transparency and fostered trust between administrators and faculty, who were now both able to see a shared vision—crucial components in leader-follower relations and organizational strategic planning (Braun et al., 2013; Shadraconis, 2013).

Comprehensive Component of ECZ Planning

Change plans must also be comprehensive and consider "a vast array of real and potential intervening variables" (Polka, 2007, p. 189). With only a week to plan in a highly VUCA environment, teams at this case study institution quickly identified the priority areas for discussion and planning.

For example, in television production advanced diploma program at one of the site colleges, the associate dean and faculty team worked to determine access to software and equipment off-campus, both of which students needed for coursework. In the insurance diploma program, meanwhile, administrators and faculty focused on how they would arrange course schedules to allow students to write industry accreditation exams as scheduled.

For the author, this left many aspects of planning to be determined, which were tackled through the summer of 2020, as was experienced at many other institutions. More time to comprehensively review scenarios may have alleviated some of the pressures and personal and professional stress experienced by leader based on this change.

Continuous Component of ECZ Planning

Organizations must also plan for change so that it is *continuous*—without a pre-fixed deadline, to allow for ongoing iteration due to contextual changes (Polka, 2007). While the semester plans would be implemented in fall 2020, the scenarios-planning provided an opportunity for colleges to adjust plans based on situational or environmental changes.

Teams at the case study colleges were encouraged to develop contingency plans for additional scenarios, including a potential interruption in the fall due to local outbreaks, and a rapid return to campus, pending government approval. This promoted ongoing thinking and adjustment to the plans. As cited by Polka (2007), "the planning process must be viewed as a *continuous* experience" (p. 189).

Concrete Component of ECZ Planning

The final need for organizational change, according to the Effective Change Zone research, is to show *concrete* evidence of the change to reinforce to team members the value of their change efforts (Polka, 2007). While plans were shared and thanks given to those involved, there was little recognition provided for the efforts of those involved at one of the author's site college. Leaders often provided initial thanks, but upon later reflection, admitted that they should have provided more check-ins and evidence to show the progress of change.

Kotter (2012) posited that celebrating wins, no matter how small, and building upon them to enact further change, are key "high-touch" steps organizational leaders are most likely to forget. Several Ontario college administrators are continuing to reflect about how they may demonstrate the proof of success resulting from those plans as a key component of the post-pandemic recovery. However, it is imperative that those leaders contine to maintain a

"People First" orientation in their analysis of their journey through the crisis at their respective organization.

Change, Communication, and Trust

As the weeks wore on during the early months of the pandemic, it became clear at many institutions that fall 2020 enrollment, particularly international enrolment, was going to suffer immensely. Travel and border restrictions had halted all international travel and visa processing had shuttered at embassies, preventing international students from arriving in Canada.

However, in the case study institutions, international students represented about 35 percent of full-time enrollment, as is typical at many colleges in Ontario. This dynamic created a significant deficit for those colleges, requiring hefty cuts to operating budgets. While some of the savings were realized through reduced course offerings, other changes were required to meet these targets.

In addition, administrative leadership teams were sometimes tasked with finding efficiencies in their operations, such as suspending low-enrolment programs, while also identifying potential opportunities for change in their program mix. There were considerable sensitivities related to this work, as program suspensions, even those that are temporary, consequently reduce teaching hours for faculty and could lead to job losses.

Therefore, it was necessary, to keep this tactical planning work confidential among administrators only. For example, in one department at one of the site institutions: three programs were suspended indefinitely, two were suspended for retooling, and three more moved to continuing education. In another program, a much-loved experiential learning lab faced closure much to the chagrin of program participants and their allies.

These changes were approved through the administrative processes but not communicated to faculty teams until the decision had been made due to the confidential nature of the final decision. Faculty teams, students, and parents were upset and outraged at the lack of input and consultation. Subsequently, administrators and their teams spent several weeks responding to concerns and complaints—time that could have been better spent on other activities.

Lack of Empowerment Impacted Acceptance of Changes

According to the Effective Change Zone Model employed by several leaders in Ontario higher education settings, addressing the professional needs of those involved in the change process are critical for implementing short-term change and its sustainability long-term (Polka, 2007). While this approach was prudent at a stressful time during the pandemic, in retrospect, in many ways it was also short-sighted.

It was generally accepted that leaders must set the conditions within their organizations so that those impacted by change are able to communicate thoughts and concern regarding the changes (Kotter, 2012). However, given the confidentiality restriction, much of the analysis and planning related to personnel changes took place in isolation, with only input and discussions based on the limited administrative views of the problems and potential solutions.

This was a dilemma for educational leaders employing the key principles of the Effective Change Zone since the related research associated with it stresses the importance of empowering members in an organization to contribute to proposed change, and have input related to providing the necessary resources to enact the changes (Polka, 2007).

Lack of Creativeness in Problem-Solving Impacted Outcomes

In addition, the lack of creative problem-solving and consultation services were exposed at one of the case study colleges when the faculty team challenged the aforementioned lab closure, and requested an opportunity to pursue alternatives on their own. This work occurred with limited input from the administrative team, as resources were also cut back, and administrators were restricted from sharing budgetary data.

That faculty team returned with a series of recommendations that reduced the maintenance costs of equipment and improved accessibility and availability of the lab to students. Consequently, the lab remained open because of this serendipitous planning activity in spite ot the original leadership team plans for closure of the facility.

While the outcome was positive, several administrators regretted that they did not initially provide the team, or other teams, space, and opportunity to creatively address such problems as perhaps better outcomes may occur.

Lack of Authentic Commitment Impacted Outcomes

In addition to allowing team members to engage in the change decision-making and process, leaders also played a key role, consistent with the ECZ model research findings, in showing authentic commitment to proposed changes and illustrating the opportunities that the changes will create for members both personally, and professionally (Polka, 2007).

The lack of consultation, in the name of confidentiality, again created problems for several college leaders during this crisis. For some administrators it became personally challenging to own the decisions made, as they felt that they would have likely chosen a different path and process if the budgetary, confidentiality, and pandemic-related urgency concerns were not factors.

It must be stated that many senior college administrators and other leaders were not necessarily sold on the organizational changes proposed at both case study institutions in the early days of this crisis. Although they tried to paint a unified vision of the future, that vision was created without collaboration from their teams, which impeded buy-in from members (Kotter, 2012). This made it harder for the leaders as well as the team members to imagine the vision and exhibit unbridled passion for the proposed changes.

In several meetings, the administrators of both case study institutions were asked to lay out the goals and objectives that they wished to see from these proposed changes designed to address the exisgencies casied by the crisis. Admittedly, several of them could not answer these questions with any great amount of detail.

However, some insightful administrators, subsequently, changed the process to enable their faculty to lead program renewal activities with established goals in mind. This is a practice that many of them have avowed to continue based on their initial negative feelings with the initial process for making-decisions during this COVID-19 pandemic that did not include a wide array of inputs from those individuals most directly impacted by proposed changes in the re-focused management of their respective institution's people, things, and ideas.

Lack of Time Impacted Outcomes

Organizational members also needed time to reflect upon, absorb and implement the changes as confirmed by the research conducted by Polka and others (2007). This cannot be understated, as many indidiviuals processed the implemented changes on different timelines. By announcing the changes with little notice, the college administration inadvertently triggered a grief cycle in many team members. Kubler-Ross and Kessler (2005) described grief-cycles as consisting of the following phases of loss: denial, anger, bargaining, depression, and acceptance.

All of those phases of the grief-cycles were witnessed in their repestice teams by educational leaders throughout the global pandemic crisis at both case study institutions. It was very apparent that ndividuals processed what was occurring at different rates and at different times which meant that their organizational managers and leaders needed to be sure to address those personal issues in an individualized fashion since a "cookie cutter" type approach would not work when so many people were at different stages of implementation.

Some faculty took to social media to express their anger. Others immediately appealed to the academic vice president. Others still refused to believe that the authorized educational leaders and administrators of the college have the designated authority to make such drastic change decisions. Emotions ran high for several weeks, and many leaders, both relatively new ones and others well-seasoned, felt torn trying to address so many personal and professional issues at one time for their team members.

Those new leaders should have been building trust and relationships during this crisis, but were engaged in following the "party approach," and were acutely aware that the lack of transparency would foster suspicion and disbelief. Several of the seasoned leaders expressed concerns that the traditional "high-touch" personalized approaches to managing people at these institutions may be adversely impacted because of too much to do and so little time to do it using a gentle human touch.

A slower socialization process that included consultation would have been a more compassionate strategy to allow time for reflection and internalization. In the name of confidentiality and crisis urgency, leaders were truly unable to authentically involve their teams in the change, making it that much harder to enact.

Managing Change Virtually

Adding to the pressures of the pandemic and budget reductions, some Ontario colleges undertook a reorganization of their academic departments. This move was made to reduce several administrative positions and cut operating costs. Three new managers, representing about 40 percent of some leadership teams, were added, along with another school. Of those three new managers, two were six months into the job, having held their positions not much longer than their administrative supervisor when the proverbial crisis "hit the fan."

Although their respective teams continued to work from home, the new supervisor had the added challenge of managing a newly formed team, in some cases, not having met new team members in person. Further, most of this specific team appeared to be on the verge of burnout because of having spent many weeks of fast-paced, emergency measures to ensure students and faculty could continue to learn and teach at the college level.

The team leader was well aware that the *personal* needs of the leadership team members, including the leaders themselves, impacted the team's ability to cope and be productive, and continue to lead others effectively as identified in the change research associated with the ECZ model (Polka, 2007). Several caring and insightful leaders sought to address these needs for both individuals and the team as a whole.

Lack of Challenge Impacts Outcomes

According to the change research, to successfully cope with change, individuals must see the proposed change as a *challenge*, rather than a crisis (Polka, 2009). This was somewhat easy in the early days, in which it appeared COVID-19 perhaps would last only a few weeks, and most individuals possessed a sense of an "ending point" to this crisis—usually the end of the Spring Semester or the Winter Semester (as it is called in Canada).

But, as the pandemic dragged on, and issues related to changes in delivery, enrolment, and budgets began to pile up for the organizational leaders. There was a corresponding slow-down in decision-making, all of which contributed to additional frustrations for leaders as well as fear and anxiety among their followers.

Senge (2006) described *reframing* as changing a person's perception about a situation. Throughout leadership team online interactions at one of the colleges, the leader strove to help the team *reframe* the problems into opportunities. For example, moving an applied course online might be a challenge, but provides a chance to try new technology, or upgrade faculty skillsets. Sometimes this management approach was met with enthusiasm and at other times, not so much.

IDENTIFYING OPPORTUNITIES IN A CRISIS

However, consistently pointing out the opportunities inherent in the challenges associated with the crisis promoted another of one of the key personal needs associated with the ECZ research model: *creativity*. By reframing their thinking, team members were able to remain open to new ideas. Organizational managers worked with their teams to find creative ways to solve problems or plan ahead at some of the colleges.

One associate dean developed a new process and form for remedial credit recovery. Another designed an innovative team-teaching approach to support larger class sizes without sacrificing student-faculty interaction. There were positive collateral impacts of this crisis in terms of re-thinking processes, procedures, and the traditional ways of doing the business of higher educaaiton management at both case study sites.

Some caring leaders focused their efforts on providing their team with supports and championing their ideas within the organization, while also clearing internal bureaucratic roadblocks. Allowing the team space and flexibility to complete this work also helped build trust and confidence, and provided a level of *control* over the changes that were to come which is another key personal need of the *Effective Change Zone* model (Polka, 2007).

Also, it became obvious to the educational leaders and imperative for the sake of the institutions that in order to appropriately establish the conditions for effective and sustainable changes, all members needed to exhibit a level of *commitment* to their work and the organization, and showed that they genuinely *cared* for one another (Polka, 2007).

As an example, one of the newly re-constituted teams, very familiar to the author, went above and beyond the expectations set for them by their organizational leaders on many occasions. They collaborated on several Sunday evenings and during late-night sessions. They communicated with the associate deans through MS Teams or other computer applications, as they worked diligently to prepare data reports or complete program plans for various stakeholders at the college.

They cooperatively shared successes and failures, and pitched in to help when another team member was underwater with demands. They regularly shared ideas, personal concerns, and professional frustrations, with each other which resulted in building acute camaraderie and an authentic sense of cohesion which was not expected of such a newly formed team.

The college leadership was very proud that this teamwork and support was occurring, despite the virtual environment. However, some administrators began to see a trend of overwork and over-commitment, including from some of the leaders. The pandemic created a sense of urgency for all and this morphed into a feeling that everyone should be working long hours and weekends to keep up with the ubiquitous and ever-relentless demands for information.

In addition, the work-at-home environments meant that casual hallway conversations had to be scheduled, leading to more and more meetings online throughout the day. The "high-touch," serendipitous "water cooler" type meetings were no longer an experience!

As many people worldwide lost employment, worry set in, and while it was not directly expressed to many college leaders, some focus team members were afraid to say "no" to unrealistic requests, in fear of losing their jobs.

However, once this became known, several key administrators worked to help team members prioritize their work, stepped in to block unrealistic requests, and used their official authority to assist with trickier problems that required help from other areas of the college. Administrators also promoted the need for team members to experience "down time" away from work during the evenings and on weekends—and especially enjoy a vacation or even a "staycation" whenever possible.

It is important to note that several leaders observed at both case study colleges modeled the behaviors that they wanted to see in their followers (Kouzes & Posner, 2006) by refraining from contacting the team outside working hours, and disconnecting from work communications as much as possible while on vacation.

During the summer of 2020, the author engaged a specific team in a strategic priority-setting exercise, which allowed them to begin to plan for the future. In this way, that team was able to mentally move out of a coping phase in which they just managed the problems of the day, toward building a plan for future development with their own teams. A refreshing change in orientation that sparked a renewed interest in future thinking.

This work was rewarding, but also draining at times for the college leaders. Many of them experienced frustration, anxiety, and self-doubt that the colleges and the entire education system would eventually emerge from this crisis, and whether individuals within the organization were skilled enough to lead a team through the worst of it.

Several leaders fought hard to "hold back" or suspend their personal emotions many times through employee conflicts, layoffs, negotiating with other departments for help or resources, delays with decision-making, and other hurdles.

The five personal needs of the Effective Change Zone identified as bedrock dispositions for change leaders: *challenge*, *creativity*, *control*, *commitment* and *caring*, applied equally to leaders, and several times, leaders commented to this author about their personal reflections of their own personal needs and self-efficacy.

Boundaries around work hours, prioritizing activity, and asking for help provided space and reassurance to allow some of the leaders to reconnect with those needs so that they could personally manage, and lead others through the unpredicatable changes that were still ahead.

However, in discussions with other leaders in different college contexts those five Cs: *challenge*, *creativity*, *control*, *commitment,* and *caring* of the Effective Change zone continued to inform their leadership practices and help them manage the people, things, and ideas of their respective educational organizaiton, especially during this global pandemic crisis.

FINAL THOUGHTS

The impacts of the pandemic on postsecondary institutions is not yet known. Higher education institutions tend to be a relatively stable sector, but COVID-19 has introduced new ways of working and learning that are likely to change institutions in major ways. Significant organizational change in higher education usually occurs slowly due to the decentralized and loosely coupled structure of the institution (Orton & Weick, 1990).

Formal or informal shared governance requires a highly consultative and inclusive decision-making process (Taylor, 2013). However, the ECZ model provided leaders at the case study colleges with an effective inclusive change model that they employed to survive and thrive in this crisis environment.

The pandemic was a cataclysmic change event for which modern colleges and universities had no precedent or parallel and the collateral impacts of it will be felt by students, professors, and administrators for years to come. Perhaps, higher education leaders truly learned a lesson via their experiences in this punctuated equilibrium that may have changed forever many of the structural and procedural traditions associated with college around the world.

While institutions had prepared for emergencies such as environmental catastrophes, cyber-attacks, school shootings, or other crises (Jiang, 2018; Wang & Hutchins, 2010), the COVID-19 pandemic differs in its global reach and longevity. No country, province or city has been spared; widespread disruption is now measured in months, if not years.

What is evident is that flexibility and adaptability needed to become institutional and personal values. Colleges and universities must learn to continue to build flexible and adaptable systems, structures, and approaches to respond to future needs of their students, employees, and other stakeholders, to ensure future survival and continued success.

For new college administrators just beginning their leadership journey, the pandemic became a trial-by-fire training ground, testing their leadership at every turn. Punctuated equilibrium often serves as the catalyst for change and learning (Romanelli & Tushman, 1994), of a breadth and depth that would otherwise take years to achieve.

Faculty and staff showed incredible capacity for rapid change, and a resilience in a VUCA (volatile, uncertain, complex, and ambiguous)-oriented crisis environment. Colleges and universities have had to reinvent many aspects of their operations, including policies, procedures, processes, and programs, in response to the new conditions caused by the pandemic.

The complexity of these changes creates immense pressures that are helped or hindered by both communication and trust between employee groups. Individuals, teams, and organizations involved in education have all learned and used new technologies and techniques to perform work tasks and teach online as well to comprehensively support students from a distance by adapting and innovating in ways that seemed impossible only months earlier.

By most measures there has been much success in re-conceptualizing educational institutions and there has been much operational success—by mid-2021, colleges were making recovery plans, and most had survived the storm relatively unscathed.

But the failures still feel raw, and some school administrators, like this author, are certain more challenges await in the years ahead. How will this pandemic change institutions, leaders, and individuals in the longer term? More research will be needed to measure the long-term impacts of one of the greatest crises in generations.

KEY PRAGMATIC LEADERSHIP
TAKEAWAYS FROM CHAPTER 7

- *Leadership is tested during crises and times of change.* Leaders must embrace the challengeshead-on through authentic communication, collaboration with team members, and by revisiting core commitments and values to help prioritize action and decision-making.
- *In difficult times, leaders need to address the personal and professional needs of their team members concurrently.* They need to be aware of the intersections of work and life for most people, and provide flexibility where possible.
- *Leaders also must balance the needs of the organization with those of individual team members.* They cannot lose sight of what the organization will need—during the crisis, recovering from it, and into the future.
- *Leading a team virtually may require high tech tools, but it also requires a high-touch approaches* (Polka, 2007). Team members need more support to navigate through new ways of working, particularly if they are new to an online work environment.
- *Leaders also need to consider their own personal needs.* Be wary of emotional exhaustion and burnout during stressful events.
- Institutions, meanwhile, need to embrace flexibility and adaptability as values that permeate all areas of the organization.

REFERENCES

Basen, I. (2019). *Ontario colleges need international tuition. It could cost them.* The Agenda. TV Ontario. https://www.tvo.org/article/ontario-colleges-need-international-tuition-it-could-cost-them.

Baumgartner, F. R., Jones, B. D., & Mortensen, P. B. (2014). Punctuated equilibrium theory: Explaining stability and change in public policymaking. *Theories of the Policy Process, 8,* 59–103.

Braun, S., Peus, C., Weisweiler, S., & Frey, D. (2013). Transformational leadership, job satisfaction, and team performance: A multilevel mediation model of trust. *Leadership Quarterly, 24*(1), 270–283.

Dennison, J. D., & Gallagher, P. (2011). *Canada's community colleges: A critical analysis.* Vancouver: UBC Press.

Drennan, L. T., McConnell, A., & Stark, A. (2014). *Risk and crisis management in the public sector*. London: Routledge.

Eagly, A. H., Nater, C., Miller, D. I., Kaufmann, M., & Sczesny, S. (2020). Gender stereotypes have changed: A cross-temporal meta-analysis of U.S. public opinion polls from 1946 to 2018. *American Psychologist, 75*(3), 301–315. doi:10.1037/amp0000494

Gartzia, L., Ryan, M. K., Balluerka, N., & Aritzeta, A. (2012). Think crisis–think female: Further evidence. *European Journal of Work and Organizational Psychology, 21*(4), 603–628.

Higgins, M., Ishimaru, A., Holcombe, R., & Fowler, A. (2012). Examining organizational learning in schools: The role of psychological safety, experimentation, and leadership that reinforces learning. *Journal of Educational Change, 13*(1), 67–94.

Jeffords, S. (2020 April 22). *Uncertain fall ahead for colleges and universities as pandemic continues.* CBC News. https://www.cbc.ca/news/canada/toronto/covid-post-secondary-1.5541556

Jiang, Y. (2018, May). Research on strategies in response to college network public opinion from the perspective of crisis management. In: *2018 4th International Conference on Humanities and Social Science Research (ICHSSR 2018)*. Atlantis Press.

Kotter, J. P. (2012). *Leading change*. Cambridge, MA: Harvard Business Press.

Kouzes, J. M., & Posner, B. Z. (2006). *The leadership challenge* (Vol. 3). New York: John Wiley & Sons.

Kübler-Ross, E., & Kessler, D. (2005). *On grief and grieving: Finding the meaning of grief through the five stages of loss*. New York: Simon and Schuster.

Marshall, J., Roache, D., & Moody-Marshall, R. (2020). Crisis leadership: A critical examination of educational leadership in higher education in the midst of the COVID-19 Pandemic. *International Studies in Educational Administration (Commonwealth Council for Educational Administration & Management), 48*(3), 30–37.

Moerschell, L., & Lao, T. M. (2012). Igniting the leadership spark: An exploration of decision making and punctuated change. *Emergence: Complexity and Organization, 14*(2), 54.

Orton, J. D., & Weick, K. E. (1990). Loosely coupled systems: A reconceptualization. *Academy of Management Review, 15*(2), 203–223.

Polka, W. S. (2007). Managing people, things, and ideas in the "effective change zone": A "high-touch" approach to educational leadership at the dawn of the twenty-first century. *Educational Planning, 16*(1).

Polka, W. (2009). Leadership in the effective change zone: A case study of the high-touch needs of educators implementing the Georgia Performance Standards. *Remembering our mission: Making education and schools better for students*, 187–199.

Romanelli, E., & Tushman, M. L. (1994). Organizational transformation as punctuated equilibrium: An empirical test. *Academy of Management Journal, 37*(5), 1141–1166.

Senge, P. M. (2006). *The fifth discipline: The art and practice of the learning organi-*
zation. Redfern, Australia: Currency.

Shadraconis, S. (2013). Organizational leadership in times of uncertainty: Is transformational leadership the answer? *LUX: A Journal of Transdisciplinary Writing and*
Research from Claremont Graduate University, *2*(1), 28, 1–15.

Taylor, M. (2013). Shared governance in the modern university. *Higher Education*
Quarterly, *67*(1), 80–94.

Usher, A., (2019). *The State of Postsecondary Education in Canada, 2019*. Toronto:
Higher Education Strategy Associates.

Veil, S. R. (2011). Mindful learning in crisis management. *The Journal of Business*
Communication (1973), *48*(2), 116–147.

Wang, J., & Hutchins, H. M. (2010). Crisis management in higher education: What
have we learned from Virginia Tech? *Advances in Developing Human Resources*,
12(5), 552–572.

Zdziarski, E. L., Rollo, J. M., & Dunkel, N. W. (2007). The crisis matrix. *Campus*
crisis management: A comprehensive guide to planning, prevention, response, and
recovery, 35–51.

Chapter 8

The Next Era Is Up to Us

Seizing Opportunities and Creating a New Future

John E. McKenna, Monica J.
VanHusen, and Walter S. Polka

"Quality is never an accident. It is always the result of intelligent effort."

—John Ruskin

The COVID-19 pandemic has been one of the worst global crises in over one hundred years. It has had profound effects on schools and has changed the way we deliver instruction and view what a day of school looks like. What once was thought as a typical day of school will never be the same, and the collective hope of educational leaders is that no one, especially teachers and students, will ever take a day of school for granted again.

But, with crisis comes opportunity, and it is imperative that the lessons learned from the experiences faced during the pandemic enable educational leaders create and advocate a new and better educational system that better meets the needs of all students and prepares them to confront the unknown challenges of their future.

In terms of creating a new and better educational system for all based on shared collective experiences of educational leaders experienced during the COVID-19 crisis, it is imperative to focus on the above words of John Ruskin, nineteenth-century English philosopher in planning for the future. Educational leaders must adroitly review and critically analyze the impact of the crisis on teaching and learning and determine the next "best fit" options for our faculty and students.

Once the "best fit" options are identified for the local, regional, state, and national levels of education, then a focused effort must be instituted to make those options the "best" options based on quality of curriculum and instruction. There must be the collective unmitigated will of educational leaders to do so, since quality is "never an accident."

The traditional classroom model and school structure has many positive aspects, and educational leaders must take the best components and build upon them to construct a preferable future that widens the opportunities for all students. The authors of this chapter understand that in-person instruction is the model that most parents and educators feel provides the best learning experiences for children. They support this premise and further believe that in-person instruction is essential for elementary students, especially in the primary grades and for special needs students who need additional individual support.

However, through this chapter's authors' personal experiences and their interactions with other educators, parents, and students, it has become apparent that there were many positive aspects associated with the new remote instructional models that were being implemented across the country.

Subsequently, educational leaders must have the courage to embrace the experiences of curriculum and instructional changes provoked by the global crisis and move forward implementing new programs and practices based on research related to those changes. It is of crucial importance for educational leaders to resist the urge to go back to the old ways and reject progress made during the crisis because it makes educational stakeholders feel uncomfortable.

Educational leaders should not back away from the positive progress that has been evidenced with technology-infused curriculum and instruction, just because it forces individuals out of their comfort zone and requires hard work to implement. The opportunity to reset to zero and recreate new systems comes around once in a century. It is time to seize the moment and re-make the experiences of the educational to a new twenty-first century view.

During the pandemic educators at all levels of the instructional spectrum were forced to rethink the way they delivered curriculum and instruction. Remote instruction and hybrid models where students were in school half of the time and home the other half became part of the new normal during the pandemic crisis. *Hyflex concurrent* models were also developed where students in school as well as at home learned together simultaneously under the direction of their teacher who was visible and accessible to all students whether directly in front of them in the traditional classroom format or remotely via technology.

To make this happen, every teacher and student needed to have a computer with a camera so they could all see each other and communicate simultaneously in real time. For this model to be most effective, each classroom should have multiple webcams, document cameras, and big screens or monitors so students and teachers can interact effectively.

These new instructional models that were initially introduced at the onset of the COVID-19 crisis greatly improved greatly throughout the pandemic, especially as teachers learned how to develop and implement interactive lessons that successfully integrated technology and better met the needs of their students. Teachers also learned how to utilize video to record lessons and design asynchronous instruction that was much more interactive and meaningful than the pre-crisis models.

In addition, teachers learned to apply and embrace the "flipped instructional model" where students were introduced to material first at home and then they, subsequently, discussed the content with their teacher in real or remote classroom settings. This "flipped instructions model' approach improved the effectiveness of the asynchronous learning model since online discussions were used to reinforce the learning of the concepts previously presented to students.

In order to provide more vibrancy and truly make this model come to life, teachers learned to develop high-quality asynchronous learning experiences utilizing, video, websites, and virtual experiences that were meaningful and personally engaging to students. This model also allowed for teachers to differentiate instruction and create individualized learning experiences based on the needs, challenges, and interests of their students. These methods also provided congruency between the learning styles of many students and the teaching styles of many educators.

This global crisis has identified that course content and concept instruction can now take place through multiple forms, in diverse modalities, and at anytime and anywhere convenient to students and their respective teachers. Such new and diverse learning experiences including, synchronous, asynchronous, in person, remote, hybrid or virtual learning have established their place in the instructional toolbox of many teachers. Accordingly, more educators recognized the significance of the perception shared by many educational leaders of the past, and specifically articulated regarding student learning in the following composition:

> All students can, in fact, learn . . . but not in the same way . . . nor onthe same day; since each student possesses special gifts and talents, and each student, also, has specific special needs.

*And, it is our professional educators' responsibility to capitalize on each stu-
dent's gifts and talents as well as to provide or their special needs as best as
we can via research-based effective instructional practices, caring approaches,
and student focused differentiation of both teaching and learning* (Polka &
McKenna, 2016, p. 10).

The widespread implementation of these new instructional techniques and
methods during COVID-19 made a major difference in the lives and learnings of many students, teachers, and parents. In fact, some students flourished
and performed better utilizing remote learning models. Since it has been
determined that students are very comfortable using technology, they quickly
adapted to using laptops, accessing material, uploading, and downloading
assignments, and creating new modalities to answer questions, interact with
peers, and engage in creative problem solving.

They could, and most frequently did, meet in small groups and work on
cooperative projects and reports together. These small cooperative groups
were flexible, and students had the ability to schedule times to meet that were
convenient for them. This expanded learning beyond regular school hours and
allowed students to have more time on task engaged in meaningful projects.
Most educators are just scratching the surface of the possibilities that can be
achieved by implementing remote learning and high-quality asynchronous
and synchronous experiences.

A significant number of parents have reported that they prefer the remote
learning model for their children because they felt that it better met their individual needs and helped relieve their children's anxiety of attending regular
school. Also, many parents preferred a remote option because their children
or family members are immune compromised, and they were concerned for
their health and safety.

Other parents felt strongly that multiple options including remote, hybrid,
or hyflex models should be permanently in place because they believe that
having this flexibility in learning choice helps them make decisions about the
model that best fits their individual children's interests and needs and would
be better for their social and emotional well-being.

Some students have serious anxiety issues and attending traditional schooling settings is extremely difficult for them. Also, there are some students with
unique special physical needs, emotional issues, or attention deficit needs that
were better addressed using remote options. Parents of these children strongly
advocate for schools to continue to offer remote options to meet the learning
and developmental needs of their children. They also expressed that it was a
safer environment to protect their children from contagious diseases and from
being bullied in traditional class settings.

There was also a segment of educators who thrived as remote teachers. The COVID crisis revealed that many teachers possess outstanding technological skills and an acute ability to design remote instruction that is engaging and meets the individual needs and interests of students. Some teachers have done a fantastic job of creating instructional videos that provide step-by-step instructions on how to learn course material, either synchronously or asynchronously.

These videos often provide real-world examples so students can see the concepts being taught in real-world type action. These videos can then be used to review and reteach material if a student needs more reinforcement of the concepts taught. Parents can also view the videos, and this helps parents to be able to provide support to their children during the learning process since impactful learning often occurs serendipitously without regard to scheduled times or contextual settings.

It has also been observed that several teachers who have implemented multiple cameras and methods in their classrooms have incrementally moved their instruction to a new level not previously imaged by them. Using multiple webcams, document cameras, and video recorders strategically placed in the room has had a profound effect on the teaching and learning experience of remote students since it makes all dimensions of the learning environment become more "real."

Some teachers have found ways to provide their students with multiple camera angles and video experiences that have made their classrooms come alive in a truly "high-touch" fashion that are the envy of the more tradition-bound classroom teachers. These ideas have so much potential and must be further explored by educational leaders who recognize that quality in instruction does not occur by "accident" but by the intelligent efforts of the teachers and their will to make a superior learning environment.

Parents and educators have also expressed the need to provide remote instruction for those students who experience a serious health crisis and for those who get suspended and are experiencing behavioral issues. In the pre-COVID world, if a student became ill or experienced a serious accident, they would be placed on home teaching and receive minimal support as they healed and went through their personal crisis.

However, because of the widespread integration of technology into teaching and learning as well as improved availability of it caused by the global pandemic, educators are now able to provide these students with quality remote instruction as they heal from home. Using the hyflex concurrent model, the student can attend class with their peers on their laptop from home and not miss a day of instruction and are also able to maintain their social contacts with their peers.

The same premise holds true for those students who are suspended for inappropriate behaviors. These students could receive high-quality remote instruction and not miss important learning experiences. It is well-documented that when students miss learning and fall behind, they become frustrated, and this can be the cause of more acting out and inappropriate behaviors. It seems counter-productive to suspend students who need to learn and not provide them with quality instructional opportunities. Thus, remote instruction is also beneficial in working with students who have serious behavioral issues.

Throughout the pandemic there have been thousands of students who have had to quarantine for multiple days and weeks as a result of having been diagnosed or exposed to COVID-19. These students have missed a great deal of instruction that may have had a negative impact on their learning progress. These situations could have been significantly diminished if all schools provided some form of remote or hyflex instructional options.

There are clearly good reasons to continue to explore how to enhance the implementation of remote instructional models. That is why it is so perplexing to many educational leaders that the prevailing message from most public-school officials is to return all students back to in-person instruction in traditional classrooms and discard implementing and exploring remote options for the near as well as long-term future. The editors of this book believe this is a mistake.

This is an opportunity to truly change the traditional system of teaching and learning that has been practiced for centuries and move teaching and learning into the next stage based on the employment of technology as a key tool in the process but with knowledgeable teachers who effectively balance the "high-tech" delivery of course content with a "high-touch" personal approach that is student-centered.

It has been stated that "Opportunities are like sunsets . . . if you wait too long you will miss it (Ward). Educational leaders are encouraged to not miss this opportunity to significantly change education to a more student-centered learning system where teaching and learning occurs at any time and in any place convenient and beneficial to students and their teachers.

It is the strong belief of the editors of this book that public education and public educators must be the leaders in innovation and change moving forward from the pandemic. The world will never be the same, and remote instruction is here to stay. It has also been the long-standing belief of the editors of this book that public education is the most comprehensive, inclusive, and best system for educating our children.

Public educators need to seize the moment and take the lead to develop and nurture these new modalities to reach more students, more effectively. If they do not seize this opportunity, others most certainly will. There is a widespread concern among educational leaders who led their respective schools and school systems through this global pandemic that change in educational operations will be promulgated from entrepreneurs and privateers outside the public education system. Their motives will be profit-driven and the continuance of a corporate agenda including the privatization of public schools.

Public education has a great opportunity to begin a new paradigm and craft a new mindset regarding the delivery of curriculum and instruction more effectively to more students. Public school educational leaders are uniquely positioned to collaborate with others in their region and across the country to develop remote courses and distance learning opportunities for all students.

A student in one district could remotely take a course in another district. This would allow students to take a variety of courses and subjects that may not be available in their home districts. This type of system would help create greater equity of educational opportunities and allow all students to find courses of study and programs that meet their individual interests and needs. Sharing services and staff would also be cost effective for school districts. They could offer more choices to students and save money on staffing and reinvest the savings into program research and development.

Districts could also continue to work together in fostering relationships with colleges and universities to offer advanced placement courses so students could receive college credits while still in high school. Courses could be broadcast directly from the college or university using their faculty or high school teachers could be trained to deliver the courses. These courses could be totally remote or employ a hybrid option where some students attend in person and others attend remotely. This type of arrangement seemed to work well in many instances during the crisis—why not in the post-crisis period?

It is also the belief of the authors of this chapter that various options for hybrid learning need to be comprehensively explored and systematically researched. The hyflex concurrent model identified in this book and elsewhere enables students in class and students at home to learn at the same time. This model works best when a classroom is equipped with the proper technology.

To make this hyflex model work, each student needs a laptop, and teachers need a variety of technology including laptops, webcams, document cameras, and big video screens in ther respective teaching stations. Teachers also need additional training in teaching concurrently, and professional learning communities (PLCs) provide an excellent venue to further develop concurrent teaching skills and materials. This model provides a great deal of flexibility for students since they can attend in person or remotely on any given day. Thus, another step in the important progression to more student-centered learning experiences for more students.

Another form of hybrid learning would allow for students to attend regular class for some courses and remotely for others. This model would give students flexibility to be both a "remote" and "in-person" student based on their choice and the courses they select. This type of model would also enable teachers who prefer to teach remotely the opportunity to develop new, creative methods to deliver instruction in meaningful ways to meet the diverse needs and interests of their respective students.

The final instructional method that was used effectively employed for many students during the 2020–2021 school year was the development of asynchronous courses where students worked at their own pace and at times that were most convenient for them. Creative teachers developed interactive, video-rich, hands-on instruction that was on a platform that allowed students to work at their own pace. These platforms also allowed for students to work cooperatively with other students on projects, assignments, and research papers.

Many colleges and universities have already implemented these models, and there is no reason that public high schools should not begin exploring these options. These methods will definitely help students become college and career ready since both the traditional higher experiences as well as the traditional work experiences were radically redesigned as a result COVID-19.

However, it is recognized that remote instruction is not for everybody and most educators agree that "in-person" instruction does have many benefits. The editors of this book definitely contend that some, if not most, students learn best when in various, well-designed, "in-person," student-centered classroom settings.

Also, there are many important reasons to attend school, including building friendships, cultivating relationships, cooperative learning, learning to work with others, direct instruction, hands-on learning, participating in extracurricular activities and interscholastic sports, and many others. But, the question that this COVID-19 crisis raised, " . . . is this best and most effective for everyone . . . as has been practiced traditionally for decades?"

However, it should also be acknowledged that remote instruction works well for some students and that its application at all levels of the instructional spectrum needs to be continuously and comprehensively explored and specifically researched. It has also become evident that some teachers are outstanding remote educators, and they have developed some outstanding lessons and units of study that meaningfully connected with their students.

Those educators, who effectively thrived as teacher leaders during this crisis, have a professional responsibility to their education colleagues to share their experiences and help their colleagues develop and foster the best learning opportunities and experiences for all students. It is also evident to the authors of chapters in this text and other visionary educational leaders that "The future is now." The COVID-19 crisis provided an unique opportunity for educational leaders to seize the moment and change traditional mindsets in order to create an educational system that works most effectively for all of our students.

The previous chapters provided valuable insights from the experiences of seasoned educational leaders who represented the various facets of school organizations and departments, they provided their candid assessments of the leadership approaches, programs, knowledge, and skills they employed to deal with the impending and continuing COVID-19 global pandemic.

The various authors of chapters in this book offered their "lived experiences" as proof that changes, caused by unanticipated crises, could be addressed, and the open-social system of schooling could continue to expand to address the multi-dimensional needs of the people served in schools and their respective communities. Whenever the new post-crisis period begins, it is imperative that future educational leaders learn from the experiences of those who have weathered the impending crisis and were able to exert control over its eventual outcomes.

Future educational leaders need to remember the lessons learned as well as the specific leadership behaviors, dispositions, and approaches articulated in the foregoing chapters that enabled those educational leaders to personally and organizationally address the enormity and rapidity of such an unexpected and rapid punctuated equilibrium as COVID-19.

Leaders must be ready to manage themselves and others in any other expected or unexpected similar crisis. They must always exhibit a "high-touch" orientation to the people, things, and ideas that are impacted and that may need to be altered due to changes caused by such crises, whether natural or man-made or even a combination of both!

FINAL THOUGHTS

It is imperative for educational leaders to keep in mind that change will always occur—sometimes rapidly and sometimes slowly—but change in the open-social system of schooling will occur, and leaders will need to pilot their organizations through turbulence, similar to the Mississippi riverboat pilot recognized by Mark Twain when he stated,

> *Two things seemed pretty apparent to me. One was, that in order to be a Mississippi River pilot a man had got to learn more than any one man ought to be allowed to know; and the other was, that he must learn it all over again in a different way every 24 hours* (Twain).

And two things seem pretty evident to the editors of this book, based on the experiences of the educational leaders who shared their experiences in the foregoing chapters:

1. An educational leader, in any crisis situation, needs to learn more than any one person should be allowed to know.
2. An educational leader must learn it all over again in a different way throughout the day.

The changes that were made to the people, things, and ideas of education during COVID-19 occurred on a daily basis and may be even more significant in the long-term for restructuring education. Educational leaders must exert their will to promulgate a new mindset to educational thinking now, as the timing seems appropriate given the experiences of the global pandemic crisis.

However, educational leaders must also be advocates for quality innovations in curriculum and instruction based on the changes experienced during the crisis that expanded the scope of traditional education and enabled even more diverse learners to survive and thrive. But quality is never an accident, so educational leaders must not only exhibit their will to make significant changes to traditional education mindsets, but they must present intelligent reasons for changes based on research and evidential experiences at the local, region, state, and national levels.

Ethical and community-minded educational leaders need to exert their influence over the analyses and discussions of long-term changes to education based on their experiences and visions so that schooling is improved for more students and differentiation of instruction, predicated on their interests and needs, can finally be truly realized in the democratic educational system of the United States. However, educator leaders are adamantly cautioned to dissuade the comprehensive dismantling and abrupt discarding of the online learning and hybrid models of teaching and learning that worked for many students during the crisis pandemic.

Educational leaders need to use as their mantra for future changes to education that old saying, "Don't throw out the baby with the bathwater." They should ubiquitously and intensively advocate that this advice be heeded by teachers, administrators, policy makers, community leaders, and parents at all levels of the education spectrum as plans are developed for post-crisis survival and successful continuance of our venerable institution of schooling.

In addition, educational leaders should reflect on another reference by Will A. Foster, a twentieth-century business executive who extended and expanded Ruskin's nineteenth-century cogent comment that quality is never an accident. Foster's more comprehensive perspective about quality should provide excellent reflective opportunities for educational leaders as they prepare to embark on the difficult and demanding task of fomenting a major long-term shift in American education based on the curriculum and instructional benefits that emerged from COVID-19:

> Quality is never an accident; it is always the result of high intention, sincere effort, intelligent direction and skillful execution; it represents the wise choice of many alternatives, the cumulative experience of many masters of craftsmanship. Quality also marks the search for an ideal after necessity has been satisfied and mere usefulness achieved.

Yes, indeed, the above reference speaks volumes about the COVID-19 educational experience wherein, "necessity was satisfied and mere usefulness achieved," nut now is the time to recognize that collaboratively educational leaders can promote better quality educational programs for all students based on the experiences of the crisis by approaching educational change in the post–COVID-19 era with high intentions, sincere efforts, intelligent directions, and skillful executions. In addition, the "new education" quality will represent the wise choice of many alternatives and the cumulative experiences of many master teachers and administrators.

Leaders who direct this meaningful change in education will assuredly recognize that the quest for quality in education is a search for the ideal vision of the future especially after the necessity of confronting the turbulence of the global pandemic has been abated. This work will be very hard for focused education leaders intent on revamping schooling in contemporary society, including curriculum and instruction approaches, that are seen as useful merely because they are traditional.

However, those educational leaders who willingly and unabashedly accept the challenges of making significant changes in the traditional mindsets for education should recall the statement by then President John F. Kennedy, who in 1962 issued that famous challenge to all Americans and provided a lofty vision for dramatic actions, while recognizing it would be "hard":

> We choose to go to the moon. We choose to go to the moon in this decade and do the other things, not because they are easy, but because they are hard. (Kennedy, 1962).

The road ahead for educational leaders in adopting and adapting the positive curriculum and instructional benefits accrued to most schools because of the pandemic crisis will be hard, but if the quality for all students improves as a result of those intelligent efforts, it will be well worth the effort and result in meaningful advances in education, just like the challenge posited by JFK, and once accomplished in 1969, resulted in innumerable benefits to contemporary society.

Educational leaders must not only advocate for intelligent changes in the procedures and the operations of schools but they must do so with both a passion and a sense of urgency and destiny as Kennedy did to join the effort and cooperatively accomplish the mission. The opportunity is now; leaders must not miss it!

KEY PRAGMATIC LEADERSHIP
TAKEAWAYS FROM CHAPTER 8

- *Leaders must embrace change:* It is imperative that the leader embrace change with a growth mindset, always seeking the preferable future for the students.
- *Don't be afraid to try go against popular opinion:* A leader must do what is right not what is popular. A true leader needs to have the courage to do what is right for the students, staff, parents, and community.
- *Strive to do what is right for all students not just some:* A leader must do everything in their power to make sure that the needs of all students are met to the best extent possible. A conscience leader does not leave any child behind and strives daily to ensure that the individual needs of all students are the driving force for change.
- *Develop multiple pathways for success:* The conscience leader is intentional in making sure that multiple modalities, courses of study, and learning experiences are developed and available for all students.
- *Be a good listener:* To gain effective situational awareness, a leader must be a good listener. They must also develop multiple ways to hear peoples thoughts, ideas, and criticisms. Forums, site visits, listening tours are all specific ways a leader can listen and gather essential information to make the best decisions.
- *Be directly involved in all facets of the work and the organization:* An effective leader is a hands-on leader. Being directly involved is essential in understanding the nature of the work that needs to be done. It is also crucial in building relationships and trust. Direct involvement and visibility is a powerful way a leader can show the organization what they believe in.
- *Develop and communicate a clear mission with a strong moral purpose:* This is imperative for the leader to motivate others to become followers. When people believe in the mission and purpose they will support the cause and go above and beyond. If a leader fails to do this the work will never be embraced and will never reach its full potential.

- *Lead with research, passion, and a sense of urgency.* Educational leaders must demonstrate intelligent procedures in making changes based on research, and they must possess the passion and sense of urgency to advocate for educational changes that improve opportunities for all students to accomplish all that they are capable of achieving via their school experiences in ways that are most appropriate for them to capitalize on their interests and needs.
- *Lead with integrity:* A strong leader will always lead with honesty and integrity. They "talk the talk and walk the walk." They make decisions that are in the best interest of students, and their actions are always based on high morals and standards. They are unifiers, and people respect their opinions even if they disagree with them. A leader must be seen as a person of integrity if they wish to make significant lasting changes in any organization. A leader earns integrity and respect everyday by the inter-actions they have and the decisions they make. A true leader makes sure that their actions speak louder than their words.

REFERENCES

Foster, W. A. https://www.forbes.com/quotes/author/will-a-foster/

Kennedy, John. (1962). We choose to go to the Moon. In *Wikipedia.*

Polka, W., & McKenna, J. (Eds.) (2016). *Confronting oppressive assessments: How parents, educators, and policy-makers are rethinking current educational reforms.* Lanham, Maryland: Rowman & Littlefield.

Ruskin, John (n.d.). BrainyQuote.com. Retrieved February 1, 2022: https://www.brainyquote.com/quotes/john_ruskin_130005

Twain, M. (n.d.). Chapter 8 Perplexing Lessons: Mark Twain, http://www.telelib.com

Ward, William Arthur (n.d.). BrainyQuote.com. Retrieved February 1, 2022: https://www.brainyquote.com/quotes/william_arthur_ward_190450

Afterword

March 2020 was an unprecedented time. All major systems globally were affected by the spread of COVID-19 and the ensuing (and continuing) pandemic—none more so than education. As schools shut down, they had to immediately pivot to a myriad of changes. Of course, schools adjusted to remote instruction, but there was so much more. School officials had to locate students and families that suddenly became out of touch. School district personnel employed a number of strategies to ensure that all families had access to the internet for school information and specific grade and course assignments and resources. The schools became the center for nutritional needs, as district resources were used to get lunches (and other foodstuffs) out to families.

A few years ago, New York State Department of Education officials used a phrase to describe the state's change to Common Core and the new Annual Professional Performance Review regulations: "Building the plane in the air." The true meaning of this term was never more prevalent in education than during the past two and a half years. School district and building leaders, literally, built the "new plane of schooling" in the air while they effectively delivered instruction, internet services, computing hardware devices, and software resources; provided food and emotional support for social well-being; and furnished countless other resources to their students so that they and their respective families, as well as entire school communities, could more easily maneuver through this crisis.

Often, through tragedy comes triumph, and this book is an example of triumph. *Coping with Educational Crises: Approaches from School Leaders Who Did It* is a veritable "how-to" on navigating the rough seas of the past two-and-a-half years in education. Editors Polka, McKenna, and VanHusen have collected an impressive team of practitioners who provide actual stories, examples, and strategies to show how out-of-the-box thinking partnered with dynamic and courageous leadership can provide a positive change to learning communities in the midst of a crisis. Additionally, the leadership demonstrated in this book can also act as a "how-to" on navigating through the continuing uncertainties of this crisis and finishing the unfinished learning that students experienced during new paradigms associated with school closures as well as rapidly developed hybrid and asynchronous learning experiences. Now, with the examples from this book, is the time to start re-imagining education and for transformational leaders to seize the narrative in that reimaging!

Thomas Payton
Principal, Roanoke Avenue Elementary School
Riverhead Central School District
Board of Directors (Zone 2), National Association of Elementary School
Principals (NAESP)

About the Editors

Walter S. Polka is currently a tenured full professor in the Department of Leadership and coordinator of the PhD program in leadership and policy at Niagara University. Previously, he was an associate professor of educational administration and coordinator of the doctoral program at Georgia Southern University, Statesboro, Georgia. He also served for over thirty-five years as a teacher, curriculum coordinator, school district administrator, and superintendent of schools in New York public schools. Dr. Polka serves in leadership positions for several national and international professional organizations and has produced numerous publications including more than fifty peer-reviewed journals and five books. He has presented his education research throughout the United States and in twenty-five countries worldwide. He has received several awards and recognitions during his career, including the State University of New York at Buffalo Graduate School of Education 2013 Distinguished Alumni Award. During his higher education career, he has served as dissertation chair to over seventy doctoral candidates, including five at Addis Ababa University in Ethiopia. His research interests include school district leadership, diversity and inclusion issues, school law, personalized learning approaches, and curriculum innovations.

John E. McKenna is an award-winning educator and national speaker from western New York. He is currently an assistant professor of educational leadership at Niagara University. In his career that has spanned over thirty-five years, he has served as an acting superintendent, assistant superintendent, principal, assistant principal, and teacher. For his professional and personal contributions, he has been recognized with several honors and awards, including: the New York State Outstanding Educator and the Friend of Education Award by the School Administrators Association of New York State; the Presidential Distinguished Elementary Principal Award from the Buffalo/Niagara Chapter of Phi Delta Kappa International, the Honorary Life Award and the Advocate in Action Award by the New York State PTA, and two prestigious Distinguished Alumni Awards by the State University of New York at Buffalo Graduate School of Education in 2014 and the University at Buffalo Alumni Association in 2021. He is also a former president of the School Administrators Association of New York State, where he served approximately five hundred school districts across New York state.

Monica J. VanHusen earned her BS in public communications at Buffalo State College, an MS in education from Niagara University, and an MA in educational leadership/administration from William and Mary College. She taught social studies at the middle school level in Stafford County, Virginia, schools for eight years and was the Heim Middle School Teacher of the Year in 2010–2011. She was appointed to the position of high school instructional technology resource teacher in 2011 and became the districtwide coordinator of instructional technology resource teachers in 2018. During the COVID-19 pandemic, she played a key role in facilitating the development and implementation of both online and hybrid courses to facilitate learning for the more than thirty thousand K–12 students of Stafford County Public Schools. She was highlighted in a 2022 State University of New York College at Buffalo Athletics Publication celebrating fifty years of Title IX and female athletic programs, as she was a Buffalo State Hall of Fame in 2010 inductee for both her college interscholastic volleyball and basketball achievements. Monica's research interests relate to integrating technology in curriculum, differentiating instruction, and school leadership. She has published peer-reviewed articles and book chapters related to them.

ABOUT THE CONTRIBUTORS

Jodie L. Brinkmann is currently an assistant professor of practice at Virginia Tech in the College of Liberal Arts and Human Studies in the School of Education. She is the program coordinator for the Education Leadership Program, serving graduate students in both the Program for the Preparation of School Principals and Supervisors (MA and EdS) and the doctorate program in educational leadership and policy studies (EdD and PhD). Previously, she was an assistant professor in the School of Education at Longwood University, serving undergraduate students in the teacher preparation program. She also served for twenty-nine years in K–12 public education, including positions as an elementary teacher, mathematics coach, assistant principal, and principal for more than eleven years.

Dr. Brinkmann's research interests include curriculum and instructional leadership, exceptional education (specifically collaboration and co-teaching), and phenomenological research investigating problems in K–12 education.

Dr. Brinkmann also works on a USAID grant specifically with 21PSTEM, working with Egyptian professors developing their STEM school principal preparation programs. She currently serves as president of the Virginia Education Research Association, is an executive board member and treasurer for the International Society for Educational Planning, and serves on the executive board for the Virginia Professors of Educational Leadership.

Carol Cash is a lifelong educator who has served at all levels of public education, both within the United States and internationally. She has been recognized as Virginia's Secondary Principal of the Year and Zama's Teacher of the Year in Japan. Dr. Cash has an undergraduate degree in mathematics and a masters' degree in guidance and counseling, both from the University of South Alabama. She received an educational specialist degree from George Washington University and a doctorate from Virginia Tech in educational leadership. She is the recipient of a research award from the Southeastern Region of the Council of Educational Facility Planners, International, and currently serves on the board of the International Society of Educational Planners (ISEP) and the Virginia Association for Learning Environments (A4LE). Dr. Cash is a professor of practice, where she served for several years as the program leader for educational leadership in Virginia Tech's School of Education. She continues to pursue research in educational facilities topics and educational leadership. She has published both nationally and internationally, and has consulted with school divisions on leadership and organizational issues.

Judge Moira "Molly" H. Cooper, Esq. is a graduate of the University at Buffalo Honors College, *summa cum laude*, and the University at Buffalo School of Law, *magna cum laude*. In addition to serving as town justice for the Town of Evans, New York, she currently works as an attorney and labor relations specialist for the Williamsville Central School District. Ms. Cooper has also previously served as an attorney practicing labor, employment, and municipal law, and as the deputy director of labor relations for the county of Erie.

Ms. Cooper's professional experience includes serving as a town prosecutor, town attorney, and litigator representing municipal interests across Erie and Monroe counties. She has successfully negotiated collective bargaining agreements with a diverse range of labor organizations including law enforcement, teachers, administrators, and support staff. Ms. Cooper also routinely assists municipal entities with a variety of human resources and contract administration issues.

Ms. Cooper's daily practice involves providing assistance to school district administrators on a wide range of contract, labor, and education law issues.

Her areas of expertise include grievance administration, arbitration, PERB, Education Law Section 3214 hearings (student discipline), and Civil Service Law Sections 71, 73, and 75.

Dr. Rubie R. Harris is currently a tenured administrator at Grand Island Central School District as the assistant superintendent for school business and finance. She also serves as an adjunct professor at Niagara University in the College of Education. In addition, Dr. Harris has and continues to serve in many leadership positions for several state professional organizations, including the New York State Association of School Business Officials and New York Benefits for Educators and Students Trust. Her involvement in different professional organizations and her PhD research has assisted in voicing the needs of public school education on state funding, tax levy limits, education policies, and changes that positively impact students and school districts.

Dr. Michelle Grimes is dean of the School of Business at Conestoga College, in Kitchener, Ontario, Canada. She began her educational career in 2007 as a professor at Loyalist College, moving from teaching to administration in 2015. Since then, she has held senior administrative roles at three institutions over the past five years. Prior to her work in the college system, she spent ten years in the media industry as a journalist and programming/production executive for various Canadian media outlets. Michelle holds a PhD in leadership and policy from Niagara University, a masters of education from the University of Prince Edward Island, and two honors bachelor of applied arts degrees from Toronto Metropolitan University. She is also a mother of three boys, and she has an avid love of cooking, books, and all things Star Wars.

Ted Price, PhD, is a visiting assistant professor in the Department of Educational Leadership and Policy Studies at Virginia Tech. His research focuses include at-risk students, leadership, change management, strategic planning, and principal and superintendent preparation. Dr. Price earned his PhD from the University of Southern California. His former positions in education include being a teacher, program specialist, coordinator, director, principal, assistant superintendent, and superintendent. He is a consultant to business and industry on change management and organizational development.

Dr. Jeffrey R. Rabey is a retired superintendent of schools and currently an assistant professor in the educational leadership doctoral program at D'Youville University. He has been in education for over thirty years and a superintendent for seventeen of those years. Jeff received his PhD in Leadership and Policy from Niagara University, with his dissertation, "The

Self-Efficacy of New York State Superintendents of Schools and their Self-Reflective Practices: A Mixed Methods Analysis." Dr. Rabey has been the president of the Western New York Education Service Council, the Erie-Niagara School Superintendents' Association and Section VI of the New York State Public High School Athletic Association. Dr. Rabey also served on the New York State Education Department Mathematics Standards Review Committee, the House of Delegates for the New York State Council of School Superintendents, and twice on the Commissioner's Advisory Council for the New York State Council of School Superintendents.

Dr. Rabey was recognized as a National Academy Foundation Leadership Fellow in 2019, received the Daemen College Distinguished Alumni Award in 2013, received the Commission on Independent Colleges and Universities (CICU) Independent Sector Alumni Hall of Distinction Award, and is a recipient of the Walter Klein American Legion Post #514 Humanitarian of the Year Award. Outside of the academic world, Jeff is an avid marathoner and cyclist and was a participant in the 2019 and 2020 Empire State Ride; a five hundred-plus mile fundraising ride for Roswell Park Cancer Institute across New York State. Jeff is the husband of Tracy and proud father of Ella and Cora.

Peter DeWitt (EdD) is a former teacher (eleven years) and principal (eight years) who facilitates workshops and provides keynotes nationally and internationally focusing on leadership, coaching, and fostering inclusive school climates. DeWitt's work has been adopted at the university, state level, and national level, and he works with numerous districts, ministries of education, school boards, regional and state organizations, where he trains leadership teams and coaches building leaders.

Peter is the author of several books, including *Collaborative Leadership: 6 Influences That Matter Most* (2017), *School Climate: Leading with Collective Efficacy* (2017), *Coach It Further: Using the Art of Coaching to Improve School Leadership* (2018), *Instructional Leadership: Creating Practice Out of Theory* (2020), *Collective Leader Efficacy: Strengthening Instructional Leadership Teams* (2021), and *De-Implementation: Creating the Space to Focus on What Works* (2022).

His articles have appeared in education journals at the state, national, and international levels, and he has presented at forums, conferences, and panel discussions at state, national, and international conferences. Some of the highlights has been to present for the National Association of Elementary School Principals (NAESP), ASCD, and NBC's *Education Nation*.

Thomas Payton currently serves on the board of directors for the National Association of Elementary School Principals, representing principals in Zone 2, which includes the states of New Jersey, New York, and Pennsylvania.

For the past eighteen years, he has also proudly served as the principal of Roanoke Avenue Elementary School in the Riverhead Central School District on the East End of Long Island, New York. Tom currently resides in Riverhead, New York, with his amazing wife Holly, who teaches third grade in the Riverhead Central School District, and their three children, Benjamin (twenty), Kaya (eighteen), and Sean-Michael (sixteen), as well as their rambunctious goldendoodle, Marlo.